CONTINUOUS CITY PLANNING

Books by the Same Author

Federal Aids to Local Planning (Editor), 1941
Urban Planning and Public Opinion, 1942
Aerial Photography in Urban Planning and Research, 1948
The Corporate Planning Process, 1962
Planning: Aspects and Applications, 1966
Selected References for Corporate Planning, 1966
Comprehensive Urban Planning: A Selective Annotated Bibliography with Related Materials, 1970
City Planning and Aerial Information, 1971
Urban Air Traffic and City Planning: Case Study of Los Angeles County, 1973
Planning Urban Environment, 1974, Russian Edition, 1979
Urban Planning Theory (Editor), 1975
Comparative Urban Design, Rare Engravings, 1830–1843, 1978

CONTINUOUS CITY PLANNING

INTEGRATING MUNICIPAL MANAGEMENT AND CITY PLANNING

MELVILLE C. BRANCH
Professor of Planning
Associate Director
School of Urban and Regional Planning
University of Southern California

Illustrated by the Author

A Wiley-Interscience Publication

JOHN WILEY & SONS, New York • Chichester • Brisbane • Toronto

Library of Congress Cataloging in Publication Data:

Branch, Melville Campbell, 1913–
    Continuous city planning.

    "A Wiley-Interscience publication."
    Includes index.
    1. City planning—United States. 2. Municipal
government—United States. I. Title.

HT167.B67   352.9'6'0973   80-29368
ISBN 0-471-08943-5

Printed in the United States of America

10 9 8 7 6 5 4 3 2 1

A problem that strikes one in the study of history, regardless of period, is why man makes a poorer performance of government than almost any other activity.

Barbara Tuchman
The New York Times Book Review, July 27, 1980

Continuous planning is needed for the conservation and wise development of our national resources—both natural and human. With new inventions, new ideals, and new discoveries, no fixed plan or policy will suffice; for any rigid mold or blueprint plan, if strictly adhered to, may restrict our freedom rather than enlarge it. We must constantly make new plans to meet new conditions.

U.S. National Resources Committee
Planning Our Resources, 1938

The process is itself the actuality, and requires no antecedent static cabinet. Also the processes of the past, in their perishing, are themselves energizing as the complex origin of each novel occasion. The past is the reality at the base of each new actuality. . . .

Every occasion of actuality is in its own nature finite. There is no totality which is the harmony of all perfections. Whatever is realized in any one occasion of experience necessarily excludes the unbounded welter of contrary possibilities. There are always "others" which might have been and are not. . . .

Alfred North Whitehead,
Adventures in Ideas, 1933

PREFACE

Cities will be a critical concern in the United States and throughout the world for a long time to come. In more and more of them the birth rate exceeds the death rate. The flow of rising populations from rural to urban areas continues in most parts of the world, dramatically increasing the number of large-size urban places. Were the forces toward further urbanization to cease tomorrow, the many problems confronting cities would remain.

The problems created by this urbanization are serious. Large sections of our bigger cities are physically and socioeconomically deteriorated; some of these areas are veritable wastelands. In many municipalities in the United States, the underground utilities which make such urban concentrations possible are wearing out and must soon be replaced at enormous cost. In developing countries where rapid urbanization is taking place, many communities are entirely lacking in the public works required for healthful urban conditions. Affordable housing is scarce or nonexistent for uncounted millions of city dwellers—so much so that illegal squatter settlements exist in the larger cities of Central and South America, the Middle East, Africa, and Southeast Asia. Social services provided by municipal bureaucracies are frequently inefficient or otherwise inadequate to meet human needs. Social discord and unrest are much in evidence, as each day's news attests. Protection of persons and property becomes more difficult and expensive. Various sources of pollution contaminate the urban environment and impair its amenity. And economic and financial limitations, together with widespread overconsumption of natural resources, preclude early attainment of the growing list of great expectations suggested by the mass media and often promised by politicians.

Each of the many organizations, groups, and individuals with particular urban concerns has reasons for criticizing city planning as it is now practiced. Some people will always be dissatisfied with city planning because it involves concentrations of population with competing interests and conflicting convictions concerning the role of municipal government in directing the affairs of the city.

The mounting criticism of city planning is also the result of fundamental flaws in the concept and conduct of this activity. Unless these flaws are acknowledged and constructive actions are taken toward their elimination in both theory and practice, city planning cannot and will not contribute significantly to the gradual improvement of urban conditions.

City planning will be even less influential than it is today if it persists in what might be called its historical hangover of wishful thinking and if it continues to engage in the "seven deadly sins" described in this book. Unless this changes, city planning will be associated with management science, public administration, systems engineering, or some other field of knowledge and professional practice that gives promise of greater effectiveness.

As the subtitle and contents of this book suggest, city planning and municipal management must be integrated. The longer-range strategies, policies, and planning which are the purpose of city planning must grow out of the ongoing, shorter-range, operational planning which is the concern of public administration.

The type of continuous planning that should emerge from this amalgamation is described. Also explained is the mechanism of analyzing, planning, and evaluating results which is needed to conduct the new form of city planning. The conceptual, analytical, and procedural advances required are entirely feasible. Where there is the political will, there is the way.

It is believed that this subject matter is of interest to professional city planners and to other practitioners directly involved in planning cities: engineers; urban economists; lawyers; information specialists; political, management, and social scientists. It should also concern members of municipal legislatures, mayors, city managers, and other officials who make the governmental decisions that direct municipal activities for the body politic and in the public interest.

It is hoped that the criticisms and conclusions contained in this volume will be considered by informed private citizens and voluntary organizations active in some aspect of city planning, as part of their vital role in the gradual improvement of municipal management. Land development companies and many other private organizations and individuals closely involved with city planning will agree with the criticisms of current practice contained in this book. But private enterprise may still prefer city planning that is less rather than more effective.

The process of continuous planning is applicable to local, regional, state, and federal governmental activities which are not concerned with cities but with other jurisdictions or applications of planning, both public and private. The analytical mechanism for city planning described herein can serve the purposes of other planning endeavors.

Since this concept of continuous city planning is a product of the author's long-time study of the process of planning and his experience in several different forms of this activity, he bears sole responsibility for the thoughts and conclusions expressed. These have been progressively developed over a period of years in several professional papers, chapters of books, and a monograph. The subject has been included in several of his classes at two universities. Most recently, as a final test, the author presented the concept at the annual meeting of a state chapter of the national association of professional urban and regional planners.

MELVILLE C. BRANCH

Los Angeles, California
January 1981

CONTENTS

ILLUSTRATIONS

CONTINUOUS CITY PLANNING

INTRODUCTION

The author's conviction that there must be fundamental change in traditional city planning if it is to significantly affect the development of cities today is a consequence of his many years of study, observation, and experience in connection with several different applications of planning. These activities are reported or reflected throughout this book.

The concept of the city planning center required to conduct a new form of city planning was first suggested by the combat information centers of aircraft carriers, which the author observed as a naval officer during World War II. The number and speed of modern military aircraft made minutes critical to successful carrier operations, requiring real-time display and immediate analysis of essential information concerning what was happening in the air and on the sea. Carrier operations became so complicated, technical, and fast acting that a special instrumentality was necessary to direct these operations.

The center incorporated maps of geographical areas showing air routes to and from primary and secondary targets, larger-scale maps identifying known defenses, lists of available aircraft and crews, weather forecasts, a continuous radar plot of the location and movement of friendly and enemy aircraft and ships, and other information needed to carry out military missions. The necessary communication equipment was at hand, and a room nearby contained auditorium-type seats for pilots waiting for the signal to "scramble" and launch planes immediately. (Figure 15 on page 156 shows part of a combat information center.)

Since then, such centers have been established for intercontinental ballistic missiles, strategic aircraft, nuclear submarines, orbiting satellites, and other military systems. And private enterprises such as utility companies, oil refineries, large chemical plants, and manufacturers with automated production lines have developed their own sophisticated centers for operations control rather than *planning*.

Some years after World War II, the opportunity arose for the author, as Corporate Associate for Planning (West Coast) for Thompson Ramo Wooldridge, Inc. (now TRW), to create two corporate planning centers and to write the first book on comprehensive corporate planning, for the American Management Association (Branch, 1957, 1962). Several illustrations in the present book and a number of the techniques suggested for city planning are derived from the author's instructive experience of planning for a large diversified company engaged in automotive, electronic, and aerospace research, development, and manufacturing. He was able to apply this knowledge later as a consultant for the design of a planning center for the Aircraft Division of Douglas Aircraft Company.

At the time of the author's association with the company, TRW was the prime contractor for the technical development and managerial direction of the Intercontinental Ballistic Missile (ICBM) program. This mammoth effort, involving directly and indirectly hundreds of thousands of people and billions of dollars, produced the U.S. ICBM system required to counter the comparable military system under development in the U.S.S.R., an outgrowth of the V-2 rocket launched against England by the Germans during the last years of World War II.

As probably the largest and most complex military program undertaken by the United States up to that time, development of the ICBM system required extensive planning, including a planning center larger but basically similar to those for corporate planning. The intellectual and technical content of the program was high because of the enormous difficulties of the task and because no comparable system had previously been designed and built. Hundreds of outstanding scientists, engineers, and other specialists in dozens of different fields were involved.

After seven years with TRW, the author was appointed a member of the Board of Planning Commissioners of the City of Los Angeles (City Planning Commission). It was soon apparent that, although there are significant differences between a corporation and a municipality, there are many more similarities than dissimilarities in the *analytical process* of planning successfully for both organisms.

Certainly a city is intrinsically more diverse and complex than a corporation, ordinarily larger in size, and has a far more heterogeneous population. Sizable cities in the United States comprise a checkerboard of thousands and even many hundreds of thousands of separately owned or controlled parcels of land. A corporation normally owns or leases all of its far fewer properties. Goals and objectives are much more difficult to establish that are responsive to the body politic rather than to the directors and owners of a business. Political, social, cultural, and ethnic factors are more directly of the essence in city planning and are at the same time more complex and capricious. Many more conflicting and special interests must be resolved; many more pressure groups must be dealt with directly.

Despite these differences, the analytical process of planning for both organisms involves the same major elements and methodologies: collection and processing of diverse information; statistical, mathematical, and other analysis of data; reliable simulation of the organizational entity being planned; projection into the future; flexible display of information and analysis for decision-makers; formulation of objectives and programs of accomplishment; and feedback to effect changes and improve performance.

Perhaps the main difference between a corporation and a city is that business planning is faster acting, but this difference may diminish as big businesses become more bureaucratic and cities become more critically dependent on reliable and rapidly responsive physical utility, social service, and other municipal operating subsystems. And as the size of large corporations increases and they are subject to more and more restrictive laws and regulations, political and social demands, and national and international conditions and events, the substantive differences between planning for smaller municipalities and larger corporations become more different in degree than in kind.

Soon after his appointment as a city planning commissioner in 1961, the author proposed a "Master Plan Reference" for Los Angeles: an installation comparable to the corporate planning centers developed for TRW and Douglas Aircraft, and precursory to the analytical mechanism that is the subject of this volume. The conviction that a new instrumentality of city planning, incorporating a new form of master plan, was needed evolved during the first year the author was on the City Planning Commission. It was immediately apparent to him that something was fundamentally wrong with the urban planning process as conducted.

Incomprehensibly, the City Planning Commission and Department had little or nothing to do with planning by the municipal departments that conducted the operational activities of the city: protection of persons and property, public works, transportation, utilities, recreation, and social services. So-called city planning had no relation to the revenue collection, and financial and budgetary processes that provide the funds for anything to be accomplished. Its sole significant concern was land use, subject to the separate actions or desires of the operating departments over which it had little or no control, and subject to the independent and usually purely political actions of the city council.

Even land-use planning by the City Planning Commission and Department was more pretense than meaningful reality. When requests for changes in existing land-use zones were considered—and during the peak period there were some forty considered in a single afternoon's session devoted to zoning—it was obviously desirable to compare them with the land use proposed on the master plan: a large leather-bound atlas resting on a table in front of the commission showing recommended land uses in different colors applied with grease pencils.

As the weeks went by, changes in land use that differed from the master plan were recommended by the commission and enacted by the city council, or granted by the council contrary to the recommendation of the commission. Many of the council's contrary actions were not regularly reported to the commission. These differences in zone between what was shown on the plan and the land use that was approved were not recorded immediately on the master plan by corresponding changes in color. As a consequence, the plan became progessively more out of date as decisions accumulated that differed from what it proposed.

At first, commission members could remember many of the changes in land use they voted on that differed from the master plan. They could make their own mental correction as they referred to the outdated, inaccurate master plan before them. But there were actions by the commission when every member was not present. And there were the changes in recommended land use made by the city council that the commission did not know about until long after they were made. Soon the differences were so numerous that remembering all of them was impossible.

It was not long before the commission referred more often to a zoning atlas published by a private firm, showing *existing* land use updated once a year, than to the master plan prepared by the planning department. When asked why the master plan was not up to date, city planning staff repeatedly assured the commission that it was being worked on "upstairs" and would be forthcoming soon. When the author left the commission nine years later, the master plan atlas was still "upstairs": hopelessly out of date as well as entirely inadequate in content.

This was in sharp contrast with corporate planning as the author had experienced it previously. In the business world, no significant changes affecting operations and profitability can be ignored without threatening the success of the company, as well as the careers of the executive decision-makers responsible for directive management. The body of descriptive information and analysis they use must be up to date. It must reflect immediately the impacts of significant events: a substantial addition to or subtraction from the sales backlog, an important customer threatening to take his business elsewhere, changes in the cost of borrowed money, labor strife, a major technological advance, or any one of dozens of possible occurrences.

Admittedly, comprehensive planning of any kind is difficult to establish because fundamental managerial advances involving top officials and executives do not come about naturally from within public or private organizations. Usually they result from external conditions and internal problems that force managerial advancement, rather than from initiative on the part of progressive decision-makers. "Politicians have seldom been leaders" (Lamm, 1980); nor are decision-makers in private enterprise prone to jeopardize their position by promoting managerial innovation, unless required to by circumstance.

It is important at this point to clarify a common misapprehension concerning "comprehensive planning." Almost since the first use of the term, many people have assumed that it means taking into reliable analytical account *every* element and aspect of the organism involved. Therefore, they conclude correctly that comprehensive city planning is impossible by definition, since it is inconceivable that all elements and aspects of a city can be identified and correlated analytically with each other. We know enough of the intricate and perhaps limitless complexity of the "simplest" organisms to realize that total analytical understanding of entireties as complex as cities is impossible now and will not be possible for a long time to come, if ever.

> The concern about comprehensiveness is misplaced because the real problem in decision analysis is not making analyses complicated enough to be comprehensive, but rather keeping them simple enough to be affordable and useful. . . . The problem is not creating complexity but retaining informative simplicity. (Howard, 1980)

The dictionary defines "comprehensive" as: "Including much; comprising many things; having a wide scope. . . ." Neither the definition nor the process of comprehensive planning imply that total planning is possible or even desirable—that "every single thing" is included. Comprehensive planning seeks to include in its scan of consideration, analysis, decision-making, and directive management as many elements as knowledge, circumstances, time, and cost permit. It cannot accomplish more than is possible within the limits established by human capabilities, the development of the organism in the past, its inherent characteristics, resources, momentum, and the external environment within which it functions. It is as important for city planners and decision-makers to recognize and accept these limits as it is for them to identify potentialities. (Branch, 1977)

Accurate use of the term differentiates comprehensive planning which incorporates as many elements and aspects of the total system as possible, from functional planning which has to do with one of its elements and from subsystem planning which has to do with several closely related elements. However, any single function or subsystem of a larger organism can itself be planned comprehensively, since it too has multiple parts. Theoretically, only the ultimately small element could not be conceived and planned comprehensively.

As would be expected, comprehensive planning at the topmost level of business management has developed faster than comprehensive city planning. "Corporate planning" is now a recognized part of business management, an established activity in one form or another in most large American companies.

> More companies are expanding planning staffs, which try to determine the shape of the future and how companies should respond to it. Of 300 large companies surveyed . . . 54% increased their planning staffs. . . .
>
> The survey also showed that planning staffs' responsibilities had changed at 70% of the companies, with 90% of those bolstering the planning function. . . .
>
> 53% of the companies will increase their planning staffs during the next two years. (*The Wall Street Journal,* 1979)

The American Institute of Management Sciences (TIMS) and the Operations Research Society of America (ORSA) have had corporate planning sections for many years. As long ago as 1961, the same year the author began his nine years as a city planning commissioner, he was a founding member of the TIMS College of [Corporate] Planning in Los Angeles.

In cities, comprehensive planning is much less advanced. The top municipal decision-makers are elected legislators who, for political reasons, do not want to commit themselves through comprehensive city planning to anything more than absolutely necessary. Some are less concerned with proper performance in their present position than with using it as a springboard to higher elective office. Nor, unfortunately, does the electorate value in their political representatives the personal qualities and actions required for competent comprehensive city planning, as much as they judge them according to: "What have you done for me lately?" There is no compelling motivation as yet for the topmost municipal decision-makers to undertake, much less embrace, comprehensive city planning.

But certain forces are changing this situation in the United States. More and more, the public is insisting that municipal utilities and city services be provided without the inefficiencies that raise costs and cause people severe problems, or the breakdowns that can bring about urban catastrophe. Proposition 13 in California and comparable legislation in other states signify the serious concern of at least property-owning tax-payers with the cost-effectiveness of local government. People are reacting to the increase in public spending by the main industrialized countries from 28 percent of national output in 1955–1957 to 41 percent by the mid-1970s (Hershey, 1979).

The federal government, with its "carrot" of proffered support and the "stick" of assistance withheld, has continued its deliberate efforts over many years to improve the capabilities and performance of local government and city planning. The allied professional field of public administration contributes to better government, and each new generation of trained public administrators improves the quality of public management. Technological advances such as computer analysis, electronic graphic display, and remote sensing call for increasing supervisorial competence.

As a consequence of such developments, many municipal departments have markedly improved the planning of their own activities. But their planning must be integrated into the total citywide "system" of which they are only one part if the city is to function effectively. It is this highest level of integrative or comprehensive planning that has not yet been achieved.

There is no doubt in the author's mind that unless effective comprehensive city planning is realized, urban disruption and social chaos will occur sooner or later. The conviction of this need—if not of the potential consequences—is shared by more and more members of the urban and regional planning profession. The immediate requirement is to determine how this improved city planning, which the author calls *continuous city planning,* can be inaugurated, what analytical methods are to be employed at its inception and what operational mechanism is to be used.

This will take time, because fundamental changes in attitude, motivation, and activity are required on the part of the governmental decision-makers responsible for directing cities. Some time in the future, city planning procedures comparable to those described in this book will be established in an American city. After a period of trial and error, its success will be noted by other municipalities. Gradually, pressures will develop for cities generally to adopt the new procedures required to manage increasingly complex urban organisms and to avoid governmental inefficiency, waste, or breakdowns, which the public will not tolerate indefinitely. (Note 1)

NOTE

1. Portions of this book are adapted from: Melville C. Branch, "Continuous City Planning," PAS Report No. 290, Chicago, Illinois (American Society of Planning Officials), 1973, 26 pp.; "Continuous City Planning," Chapter 11, *Planning Urban Environment,* Stroudsburg, Pennsylvania (Dowden, Hutchinson & Ross), 1974, pp. 203–248; "Continuous City Planning," Chapter 18, *Urban Planning Theory,* Stroudsburg, Pennsylvania (Dowden, Hutchinson & Ross), 1975, pp. 240–251.

REFERENCES

Branch, Melville C., "Conceptualization in Business Planning and Decision Making," The Planning Control Room of the Ramo-Wooldridge Corporation, *Journal of the American Institute of Planners,* Spring 1957, pp. 13–22.

Branch, Melville C., *The Corporate Planning Process,* New York (American Management Association), 1962, 253 pp.

Branch, Melville C., "Limits to Comprehensive Planning," *Geoforum,* Vol. 8, No. 3, 1977, pp. 99–111.

Hershey, Robert D., Jr., "Europeans Losing Faith in Public Spending," *The New York Times International Survey,* 4 February 1979, p. 11.

Howard, Ronald A., "An Assessment of Decision Analysis," *Operations Research,* Vol. 28, No. 1, January–February 1980, p. 8.

Lamm, Richard D. (Governor, State of Colorado), quoted in *Science,* Vol. 208, 2 May 1980, pp. 477–478.

The Wall Street Journal, Vol. C1, No. 104, 27 November 1979, p.1.

Part One

LEGACIES FROM THE PAST AFFECTING CITY PLANNING

As is true for all physical conditions and human situations, present-day city planning is rooted in its past. What is past is indeed prologue. Forces and attitudes present today are the result of millenia of historical development. Bearing this background in mind clarifies and explains the shortcomings of city planning as it is now conducted in the United States, provides a perspective that helps to identify improvements that can and should be made, and suggests how best to achieve constructive change.

This historical background may be familiar to recent university graduates who have taken a course in urban and regional planning or in urban studies. It is certainly less fresh in the minds of practitioners who have been preoccupied for years with problems that require for the most part only limited historical study and involve subject matter requiring very different ready recall. And the fixations and trends that have been established in city planning in the past are completely unfamiliar to most people in public administration, scientific management, engineering, social sciences, law, and other fields closely related to city planning as it is unfolding today.

PHYSICAL PLANNING

City planning dates back archaeologically at least 8000 years, to a "city plan" delineated on a wall in the settlement of Çatal Hüyük in southern Turkey, showing the geography of the site and the placement of some eighty boxlike dwellings. If any ordered arrangement of structures on the ground can be considered city planning, then city planning begins much further back in history.

In early primitive times after the discovery of fire, huts built of flammable materials were spaced far enough apart to prevent all of them going up in flames if one caught fire, as was likely to occur with open hearths. This separation of dwellings, still to be seen in primitive communities, was one of the earliest examples of the kind of provision incorporated in municipal building and safety codes today. Tradition indicated the proper placement of the chief's dwelling, and of the community meeting place or council chamber when such a communal structure was needed.

From the beginning of history the physical aspects of communities have received careful attention. Early humans were keenly aware that survival depended on physical security: shelter from which to venture forth, protection from predators and from conflagration. Awestruck by the overpowering impacts of an incomprehensible world, with its glaciers, earthquakes, volcanic eruptions, storms, floods, lightning, and astronomical events, primitive people developed magical, superstitious, and religious beliefs to withstand these frightening forces.

The functional requirements of everyday activities have always shaped the form and arrangement of communities. Unless some feature of the site restricted access from one or several directions, paths radiated outward from the center of the community in four directions roughly 90 degrees apart, providing the quickest access to all parts of the surrounding countryside and only four established routes to defend against outside attack. Most primitive communities and many cities during recorded history were approximately circular, because this geometric shape enclosed the most space within the shortest perimeter. This was important because building and maintaining perimeter protection, be it a thicket of thorn branches, a palisade, or a masonry wall, required great labor and considerable time, not only when the perimeter was first constructed but whenever it was moved outward to enclose more space for the growing community. A minimum amount of open space was required for normal everyday activities and circulation. Circulation requirements determined the amount and disposition of this form of open space. Conversely, the advantages of providing minimum space in which attackers could fight and maneuver sometimes led to making the entrance routes into the city deliberately tortuous and narrow, to prevent the attacker from quickly reaching the heart of the city.

Religious beliefs have also influenced the physical form and character of communities throughout history, directly, through the designation of hallowed ground and processional ways and the placement of religious structures. Indirectly, they shaped the physical city to the extent that they affected activities, habits, and choices of daily life that had spatial consequences.

Before 2500 B.C., the workers' town of Kahun at the Egyptian pyramid at Illahun was constructed in rectangular form, with separate and unequal quarters for officials, foremen, and workers. And much later, many Hellenistic colonies along the shores of the Mediterranean were laid out in rectangular form, even on irregular terrain requiring streets running up and down hills—some, like those found in Priene in Asia Minor, so steep that wide steps were an integral part of the street. One reason for such subdivision into rectangular lots of equal size was to facilitate the equitable allocation of property among several hundred colonists.

From earliest times and until relatively recently, both "city plans" and "city planners" have been concerned with the physical arrangement of streets, structures, and land use in space, as directed by the ruling or controlling authority, royal, religious, military, or secular as the case may have been. Political, military, economic, social, and other considerations were taken into account, if at all, by the higher authority to whom the planner reported. Since so much of past history has been directed by absolute authority, many issues that must be considered today were ignored or arbitrarily decided in the past. The city planner could realize a large-scale urban project-plan more easily and swiftly than is the case today, mainly because these project-plans were conceived, drawn, and effectuated as decreed by ruling authority.

An extreme example is Czar Peter I (Peter the Great) of Russia, who populated St. Petersburg by means of two imperial orders in January 1712 and June 1714. The first required 1000 gentry, 1000 merchants, and 1000 craftsmen to move with their families to his "new town"; the second commandeered 350 noblemen, each having 100 peasants in his possession, 300 merchants from the upper and lower classes, and 300 craftsmen from all trades. If we assume an average of four persons in the families of noblemen and merchants, and five in the families of peasants and craftsmen, Peter the Great was placing an imperial order for 120,500 people. (Egorov, 1969)

ARCHITECTS/ENGINEERS: CITY PLANNERS IN THE PAST

Since city planning has been concerned historically with carrying out physical/spatial plans, most city planners have been architects or engineers. City planners were usually architects when aesthetic aspects or large architectural projects were involved, in what today would be called "urban design" and architectural "project planning." When defensive fortification, water supply, drainage, waste disposal, or difficult site conditions were primary concerns, the city planner was usually an engineer. Often, one person acted as both architect and engineer, until each profession encompassed so much particular knowledge that the two fields required separate training and full-time application.

The list of architect city planners is long, beginning with Hippodamus of Miletus. According to Aristotle, writing in the fourth century B.C., he was the first Greek architect to practice city planning. Aristotle credits him with introducing the rectangular arrangement of broad streets crossing at right angles, and with combining the different parts of a community into a harmonious whole around the central *agora,* or marketplace. He is believed to have planned Piraeus, the harbor town serving Athens, in this rectangular pattern in 446 B.C., and one year later the Athenian colony of Thurii on the Gulf of Tarentum, south of Naples.

Several hundred years later, the Roman architect and engineer Marcus Vitruvius Pollio (known as Vitruvius) considered himself a builder of cities rather than of individual buildings. He was concerned in his writing with the following urban matters: the importance of determining site conditions before founding a city; ideal city size; the geometric efficiency of a circular urban wall; the orientation of streets with respect to prevailing winds; the location and size of the central open space or forum; the relationship between the vertical height of buildings and the horizontal distance between adjacent structures; and specific designs for cities with a coordinated arrangement of diagonal and rectangular streets and a series of open spaces of city squares. Vitruvius anticipated "our modern demand for city planners who can co-ordinate the work of men in the professional fields of architecture, landscape architecture, and engineering when he says of the different branches of the art and science of city building: 'It is not important that preëminence in each [branch] be gained, but he [the planner] must not, however, be ignorant of the general principles of each' " (Adams, 1935).

Vitruvius' *De Architectura Libri Decem* (*Ten Books on Architecture*), rediscovered 1400 years after they were written, greatly influenced many architects during the classical revival in the fifteenth and sixteenth centuries. Among these was Michelangelo Buonnarroti, sculptor, artist, and architect and designer of public spaces and monumental groups of buildings in Rome for a succession of popes, and of fortifications and streets in Florence for the signori, the city's governing body. At about the same time, Leonardo da Vinci, incomparable artist, scientist, inventor, architect, and engineer, "dealt in his notebooks with the city proper, suggested the separation of pedestrian ways from heavy traffic arteries, and went so far as to urge upon the Duke of Milan the standardized mass production of workers' houses. But despite these pregnant suggestions, his contributions to the art of city building remain meager and incidental compared with his extraordinary zeal in improving the art of fortification and assault." (Mumford, 1961)

In the far east, the ancient Tamil classics of Dekkan provide a literary reconstruction of the planning of the ancient city of Madura in southern India during the first centuries after Christ. The location of the city to the south of the River Vaikai was prescribed as a protection against possible invasion from the north. Also prescribed were: its straight avenues oriented east-west and north-south, intersecting at a large central square enclosed by religious structures; the generally rectangular shape of the city with a moat outside the city walls into which the sewer system drained; a narrow forest planted around the city on three sides with irrigated agricultural fields beyond; and the location of the king's palace, schools, quarters for religious recluses, day and night markets, water cisterns, and districts for soldiers, musicians, artists, and prostitutes.

Madura is of particular interest because the process of planning ancient cities was rarely documented. The urban development of Madura involved the following sequence: (1) forest cleared, (2) ground leveled, (3) advisors consulted, (4) main temple and smaller temples built, (5) bazaar (commercial), car (primary processional), and residential streets built, (6) public platforms (parks) built and trees planted, (7) new cisterns (tanks) built, (8) walls and moat constructed, (9) king's palace erected, (10) city destroyed by flood, (11) haphazard growth and consequent congestion, (12) new survey ordered by ministers, (13) new master plan formulated. (Branch, 1959)

Few architects have been personally identified with the "organic" planning of existing communities that has occurred throughout history, or with the founding of new towns, called *bastides,* during the Middle Ages. Organic planning, rather than following an overall predetermined scheme, took place over many years as the result of a progression of sensible decisions concerning the physical layout of the city made by various individuals and groups as circumstances demanded.

> But toward the close of the Middle Ages, the rationale of this [organic] planning was expressed by the highly reflective intelligence of Leone Battista Alberti, in his 'De Re Edificatore' [Concerning Building Matters].
>
> Alberti was in many ways a typical medieval urbanist. In his concern for functionalism, the localization of business, curved streets, "he did no more," as [Pierre] Lavedan observes, "than register approval of what he saw under his eyes." (Mumford, 1961)

In the case of bastides, no architect was involved because their simple gridiron layouts were so regularized that each new town was almost a carbon copy of the others.

Throughout history, the defense of cities has been studied by military engineers, and sometimes by exceptional individuals who were both artist and engineer, a creative and practical combination found more often in the past than today. During the Renaissance, these military planners included Leonardo da Vinci; Albrecht Dürer of Germany; Sebastian Le Prestre de Vauban, Marshal of France and the best known of military engineers; the Dutchman Baron van Menno Caehoorn; and General Henri Brialmont, the "Belgian Vauban." Such men shaped the physical form of cities that had to protect themselves against attack, until the appearance of the exploding shell and rifled gun barrel in the nineteenth century rendered massive urban fortifications obsolete. At the peak of their development, urban defenses occupied immense areas around fortified cities. In a few instances, the "Vauban-type" fortifications extended so far beyond the city walls that they covered an expanse of ground as large as the area within the city walls occupied by its inhabitants (Branch, 1978; Horst de la Croix, 1972).

The contributions of architects and engineers to city planning in the past were as diverse as the needs and desires of the authorities they served, and their own capabilities and predilections. The French landscape architect André Le Nôtre, best known for his design of the vast gardens at Versailles for Louis XIV, exerted a lasting influence on city planning during the late Renaissance and afterwards. His long straight avenues, radiating from circles or *ronds-points* in palace gardens are reflected in Baron George Eugene Haussmann's planning of Paris between 1853 and 1870, and earlier in Major Pierre Charles L'Enfant's plan for Washington, D.C., in 1791. The extent to which architectural and even landscape architectural design was considered synonymous with city planning is indicated by the remark attributed to Le Nôtre, that he who is able to design a park can easily draw a plan for a city.

In the latter half of the nineteenth century, American landscape architects designed urban park systems that influenced concepts of desirable open space in cities. Frederick Law Olmsted is best known for his design of Central Park in New York City; Charles Eliot completed the Boston park system begun by Olmsted; and George Kessler and Jens Jensen designed park systems in Kansas City and Chicago respectively (Spreiregen, 1965).

Physical city planning was carried forward into this century by architect planners whose names are more familiar than those of their predecessors. Of these, the most widely referred to by far is Daniel Hudson Burnham, whose famous counsel has been repeated more often than any other statement concerning city planning:

> Make no little plans; they have no magic to stir men's blood and probably themselves will not be realized. Make big plans; aim high in hope and

work, remembering that a noble, logical diagram once recorded will never die, but long after we are gone will be a living thing, asserting itself with ever-growing insistency. Remember that our sons and grandsons are going to do things that would stagger us. Let your watchword be order and your beacon beauty. (Moore, 1921)

No clearer statement of the aspirations of urban architects is available: big master plans subject to little change, inspirational in nature, emphasizing beauty. The realist, however, could readily predict the uselessness of such plans.

In 1905, Daniel Hudson Burnham, the nation's foremost city planner, completed a comprehensive design for San Francisco. Reminiscent of the Paris of Baron Haussmann and Napoleon III, Burnham's plan called for broad boulevards, huge parks, terraced approaches to the highest hills, and incomparable vistas of the bay and surrounding country.

The 1906 catastrophe cleared so much of the central portion of the city that it seemed to invite immediate implementation of the Burnham plan. But, as Kahn's study shows, it was almost inevitable that San Francisco be rebuilt along lines laid down by the marketplace rather than the city planner. Proponents of the plan had never fully confronted the political implications of their vision. How were thousands of property owners to be guided, or even coerced, into shaping their individual decisions to suit someone else's idea of the common good? Only government could legitimately centralize the authority necessary to impose the plan, and the plan's supporters were reluctant to expand the powers of a government which tended to be corrupt and—perhaps worse—democratic. Although Burnham's design came to very little, the episode taught the valuable lesson that successful city planning must be an extension of politics, not an alternative to it. (Kahn, 1980)

Henry Wright and Clarence S. Stein designed the pathbreaking residential community of Radburn, New Jersey, about 1920. Clarence A. Perry conceived the "neighborhood unit" in 1927. Eliel Saarinen, the Finnish-American architect, proposed the spatial organization of urban areas into cellular units separated by greenbelts. The engineer Ludwig Hilbersheimer produced city plans, which were never realized, laid out exclusively with relation to prevailing winds, to minimize wind-borne air pollution. Charles Édouard Jeanneret-Gris (Le Corbusier) conceived large-scale rectilinear plans for the reconstruction of the central areas of

Paris and Marseille—also unrealized—which featured great skyscrapers spaced well apart, with low-density lowrise residential and commerical structures, recreational facilities, and parks and other open spaces in between and industry at the periphery. Frank Lloyd Wright built a model of his proposal to decentralize existing cities uniformly across the entire country, with every family living on an acre of land, and commerce, industry, and other activities distributed evenly in small units over the land. "Every architect dreams of building a city" (Johnson, 1979).

The brief historical summary indicates the extent to which city planning in the past was limited to physical aspects involving urban and project design by architects, landscape architects, and engineers. These historical limitations have persisted until recently. They are still the rule rather than the exception in the United States, despite today's very different conditions brought about by population growth and migration, new means of transportation and communication, scientific and technological advancements, vast increase in the amount of information and its widespread dissemination, and the increasing complexity and interdependence of human activities and organizations in general. While these recent developments have produced extensive changes in most intellectual fields and areas of endeavor, the scope and process of city planning have remained relatively unchanged. As a consequence, this activity has become progressively less effective.

UTOPIAN STRAIN

The need to aspire and dream, to counter the all-too-often harsh realities of life, has always existed for humankind. Without the capacity to hope and imagine, life would be much more difficult for most people, and unbearable for many. The formulation of Utopian urban concepts and grand designs has provided this necessary outlet for the urban planner.

Frustration is inherent in the practice of architecture and city planning, as it is in most fields of endeavor. The eye can see and the mind visualize many potential improvements in the physical city that could be realized only with great change in existing conditions and institutions, or only after several generations of persistent effort.

Throughout history, the architect/city planner has worked for higher authorities whose wishes were commands and whose decisions were final: Michelangelo for several popes, Baron Haussmann for King Louis XIV of France, Major L'Enfant for President Washington, or Daniel

Burnham for the mayor and city council of Chicago. The city planner is almost always producing under severe constraints imposed by higher authority or restrictive conditions in the real world.

Paradoxically, the analytical and evaluative aspects of the city planner's task provide him with a more complete and perceptive view of what is being planned than is usually acquired by those he serves, preoccupied as they must be with time- and mind-consuming executive concerns, duties, and activities. The city planner studies and analyzes. He proposes, but higher authority disposes. In military parlance, the city planner is "staff," not "line." He can, of course, function as a line executive if he has the desire, the managerial capabilities, and the opportunity to do so. But this means fundamental change in his activities and requires different capabilities.

Creative capability is a necessary quality for architects and engineers engaged in city planning. Otherwise, they cannot formulate effective solutions or different ways of achieving the objectives of the authorities they serve. But this creativity also increases city planners' awareness of the gap between the practicable and the possible, and extends their perceptions of the imaginable or ideal. Because they also tend to be public-spirited and socially sensitive, city planners are intellectually attracted to Utopian concepts, "perfect" solutions, or ideal designs that are also aesthetically satisfying. Whereas mathematicians can develop solutions that are not only immediately useful but have the aesthetic elegance prized by their fellow scientists, city planners, because of the nature of their work, can rarely combine in practice the conceptually beautiful and the immediately usable.

Thus ideal formulations relating to city planning have served throughout history to compensate for the frustrations inherent in planning existing communities. These idealizations are enjoyable exercises in creative thinking unrestricted by the conceptual limitations imposed by the real world, an indirect way of sustaining hope for a better future for mankind. They incorporate concepts that might be applied in city planning some day.

As long ago as the fourth century B.C., the Greek philosopher Aristotle formulated a list of desirable features of an ideal city-state: its location, physical size, the number and desirable intellectual and ethnic characteristics of its population, land use and ownership, zoning, water supply, protection from prevailing winds, the location of open market places and agricultural plots, and several aesthetic features.

As would be expected from an architect/engineer, Vitruvius was more graphic and precise than Aristotle in his formulation during the first century b.c. His ideal city was symmetrically octagonal in shape; eight radial streets connected the central market place with eight gates placed at the eight angles of the city wall. External approaches to these entrance gates were designed to expose the right (unshielded) side of the attackers to the defenders on the city walls. Other military recommendations called for an earthen rampart around the city, wide enough for a cohort to march on and with defense towers placed within bowshot of each other. The locations of temples, basilicas, theaters, farmhouses, water supplies, and public baths were selected. Vitruvius intended his ideal plan to reflect fitness and arrangement, proportion, uniformity, consistency, and economy.

These two examples illustrate the extent of detail ordinarily incorporated into Utopian concepts, although the subject matter of the detail may vary widely. In a physical/spatial plan, the details will be generally comparable to those in the preceding examples. In a concept emphasizing social elements, the details may concern such matters as community organization, educational facilities and methods, neighborhood cohesion, or provisions for economic and ethnic diversity.

In *Utopia,* issued in 1516, Sir Thomas More unknowingly created the generic term for the conceptualizations of ideal communities that have been formulated throughout history. A few examples illustrate the diversity of these formulations by architectural visionaries, architects and engineers, and social reformers. In *The Linear City,* the Spaniard Arturo Soria y Mata in 1882 imagined cities stretching linearly for several hundred miles along closely grouped utility lines. In *The New World of Industry and Society,* published in 1829, French social reformer François Fourier proposed housing 400 families in one large palacelike structure, which he called a "phalanstery." James Silk Buckingham, in *National Evils and Practical Remedies,* proposed in 1849 a glass-roofed new town called Victoria; and Robert Pemberton planned ten circular towns composing a Happy Colony in New Zealand. Dr. Benjamin Ward Richardson in 1875 envisioned a Utopia called Hygeia, or the City of Health, containing 100,000 inhabitants on 4000 acres. Hygeia would have railroads underground, no cellars under houses, brick construction throughout, small hospitals for every 5000 persons, and special housing for the helpless, the aged, and the mentally infirm. Later, French architect Tony Garnier presented in his book *An Industrial City,* written between 1901 and 1904, a detailed master plan for a new manufacturing town of 32,000 people. (Spreiregen, 1965; Mumford, 1961)

Some Utopian concepts were translated into physical reality, for example, the French town of Chaux by Claude Nicolas Ledoux in 1776; the Scotch community of New Lanark in 1799 by Robert Owen; New Harmony in Indiana by the followers of Frederick Rapp; and the Amana villages in Iowa. Most ideal new communities have not lasted any substantial length of time, or have developed very differently than originally planned. Recently, there has been a resurgence of attempts to found ideal communities in the United States, a reaction to environmental pollution and urban deterioration. They are small in size and populated mainly by young people who are unmarried, separated, or divorced. Social purposes have greatly outweighed any physical planning objectives.

Utopian concepts have been discussed at some length because of their importance in understanding the state of city planning in the United States today. Because, by definition, Utopias require profound societal changes that cannot be realized for a long time, they encourage imaginative thinking. This freedom from the conceptual restraints imposed by the real world has always tempted city planners to formulate plans for ideal communities as a temporary escape from the overwhelming difficulties and discouragements of trying to plan existing cities. New towns offer but little additional imaginative leeway because they are more restricted by existing norms than is commonly supposed.

In the past, royal and religious rulers could consider imaginative plans for the large-scale urban projects and redevelopment which they sponsored and carried out. If the project was not completed in their lifetime, it was usually finished by their successor. There was little need for the architects, engineers, and landscape architects who served these rulers as city planners to indulge in ideal formulations since there were opportunities to design imaginatively and to see these designs realized in space. If the prospective planner was not working for the ruling authority, he might as well extend his imaginative design into a Utopian idealization since there was no chance of the design being carried out.

Consequently, the city planner in the past was probably less frustrated and dissatisfied than he is today in the United States, where so little city planning is accomplished because of the adversary political system, great resistance to change, and reluctance or even refusal to accept longer-range public plans that require foregoing some benefit today in favor of the future. Rather than being a blueprint or an effective policy directive for significant action and accomplishment, master city plans today are more likely the lowest common denominator resulting from political conflict, competing special interests, and the pretense that city planning is far more effective than it really is.

This situation has resulted in—and perhaps partly resulted from—master plans that are often idealistic formulations rather than attainable projections or serious policy proposals. Master plans in the United States are conceived far into the future without relation to current conditions, budgets, available and potential resources, and means of effectuation. They can therefore be considered present-day manifestations of the Utopian strain which has existed throughout recorded history.

INDUSTRIAL REVOLUTION: ERA OF FUNDAMENTAL CHANGE

The period of Industrial Revolution in England and Europe, roughly the 100 years from 1750 to 1850, produced great and lasting changes in the societies, cities, and city planning in these countries. In other lands industrialization came much later, and some countries are only now entering this phase of their development.

The results rather than the process of industrialization are of primary interest here. The Industrial Revolution

> . . . produced mischief of which the consequences still pursued the British people in the 20th century. That revolution found Great Britain without any effective system of local government. . . . the towns were unorganized for any of the more important purposes of administration. . . . It is not surprising, therefore, that the towns which sprang up so rapidly, as the textile and metal industries expanded, were quite unable to handle the new problems, and that their uncontrolled growth made the new town life hideous and squalid. (Hammond, 1929)

With the migration of hundreds of thousands of poor rural dwellers to cities where work in the newly founded factories was a possibility, municipalities spread out into surrounding space. Without directive urban policies or city plans, this territorial sprawl was especially pronounced and spatially disorganized in England. This was in part because city walls were rarer in England than in Europe, where fortifications around cities tended to reduce disorderly development.

With the breakdown of strong royal or religious authority, cities were in the hands of a new class of industrial merchants whose primary interest was maximization of profits, with little concern for the city as a civic organism with an existence far longer than their lifetimes. Without the royal court or the clergy and their entourages, municipal administration was almost nonexistent or was ineffective as a directive force in cities during the Industrial Revolution.

Physical conditions were abominable, with families crowded into tenements and sanitation almost totally absent. Unemployment was high and the social conditions of the poor atrocious. The urban atmosphere was fouled by the smoke and soot of coal-fired furnaces. Railroads were extended into the centers of cities, cutting across the existing street pattern at the same level, without regard for the mismatches between the two transportation systems. This confrontation between railroads and automobiles on the city streets brought severe traffic congestion and the high costs of overpasses and underpasses. Industrial cities today have not yet recovered from the municipal burdens imposed during this period. (Mumford, 1961)

Today there are local legislatures and governmental bureaucracies concerned with the protection of persons and property, transportation, utilities and services, housing, education, public health, social services, recreation, environmental pollution, and the host of additional responsibilities and activities now accepted as part of local government. New and upgraded utility systems, better street and highway networks, and housing built to higher standards have improved the physical city. Greatly expanded educational, public health, social, cultural, and recreational facilities and services have improved social conditions in the city. And all of these are intended to serve the "common man" as well as the elite who were the primary recipients in times past. Nations that have achieved such urban improvements since the Industrial Revolution have reason to be proud of their accomplishments.

But urban population growth has not ceased despite declining birth rates in some countries. Within most cities, the internal birth rate still exceeds the death rate, producing a rising population from this cause alone (unless emigration exceeds immigration by an amount larger than the excess of births over deaths). Migration to cities is now a global rather than a national or local phenomenon. All over the world people from impoverished rural areas are flooding into cities in search of jobs and higher incomes. "Hewers of wood and drawers of water" are imported by industrial nations to perform the manual and menial work no longer acceptable to citizens with incomes and attitudes inimical to such work. And now a new kind of global international emigration is occurring from nations that are war-torn, politically repressive, or antagonistic toward groups of their own citizens.

In many parts of the world, internal growth and migration to cities have placed an impossible burden on housing, with lower-income residential densities not only increasing beyond legal limits set by building codes, but beyond maximum socially acceptable intensities in such cities as Hong Kong, Calcutta, Teheran, and Lagos. Squatter settlements are common in the larger cities of Asia, Africa, and South America. Construction of affordable urban housing does not match the influx of poor people from the countryside. It is estimated that one-third of urban dwellers in South America are living in squatter settlements.

Besides an insufficient supply of housing, many cities have not been able to build the utility and service systems needed to maintain a decent and healthful urban environment for their rising populations. Disruptive traffic congestion and serious environmental pollution have become endemic.

The average size of cities has increased since the Industrial Revolution. There are now many more with populations over 1,000,000. They incorporate many utility and service systems that did not exist 100 years ago. Industrial, commercial, and other activities carried on in cities today are more numerous and more dynamic because of rapid technological changes and almost instant communication. Certainly, modern cities are far more complex organisms than their urban predecessors. Because they have lost all self-sufficiency, they are also more vulnerable, not only to the cutoff of water, food, energy, and trade from outside sources, but to the cutoff of essential services by various specialized employee groups within the city. And as the built-up area of cities has spread over contiguous but governmentally separate jurisdictions, it has become progressively more difficult to achieve integrated regional planning, laws, standards, and operational coordination.

Obviously, these fundamental and far-reaching changes in the urban scene of industrialized nations necessitate change in the organization, objectives, and methods of city planning in the United States. There are few royal rulers today. Municipal legislatures, the body politic, mayors and city managers, department heads, the mass media, financial institutions, business and labor, and state and federal governments are the collective decision-makers. Urban design and physical reordering are no longer the foremost urban goals. A host of new considerations—political, economic, social, ethnic, legal, technological, and environmental—are intimately involved in city planning. Grand master plans for some far-off time, which do not relate to available resources nor means of progressive attainment, are anachronistic delusions. The urban world has changed, but city planners have not kept pace. They operate today outside the mainstream of decision-making and action relative to cities, regarded by those who manage the city more as a nuisance than a significant directive force.

CITY PLANNING COMMISSIONS

American cities shared most of the negative consequences of the Industrial Revolution, which first occurred in England and Europe. But they were saved some of the worse consequences by the great opening up and settlement of the middle and western United States, where the rewards of new land and new opportunities made the hardships of pioneering bearable. Only later did cities reach the size and densities of their European counterparts.

On the frontier, city planning was a mechanical matter, where some local authority—or anyone exercising the necessary initiative—would lay out a gridiron arrangement of streets that permitted a quick and easy division of the land within the community into closely comparable properties. These gridiron patterns were conveniently related to the cartographic subdivision of two-thirds of the country into a grid of square miles and quarter-mile sections.

In some instances, the founder had a plan on paper or in his head: Sir William Penn for Philadelphia (1682), James Edward Oglethorpe for Savannah (1733), and Brigham Young for Salt Lake City (1848). Thomas Jefferson brought home the map-plans of a half dozen European cities for President George Washington to consider as examples for the physical layout of the new nations's capital. Major Pierre L'Enfant's winning design (1791) was the most elaborate city plan of its time with a complex crisscrossing of diagonal boulevards cutting across a pattern of rectangular city blocks, numerous intersections of boulevards at park squares, and the formal composition of a spacious central mall linking the Capitol and White House.

Such accomplishments were few and far between. There was no institutionalized city planning, which, had it existed, might have produced better urban developments during this period of territorial expansion, growth of existing cities, and industrialization. "The more ignorant and poorer of the immigrants stayed in the cities of the eastern seaboard and provided the opportunity for speculative operations that eventually brought about slum conditions of the worst type" (Adams, 1935). In addition to large slum areas, poor sanitation, environmental pollution, deteriorated dwellings, and visual ugliness were the order of the day in most large cities. For the most part, municipal governments were grossly inefficient, many of them blatantly corrupt. None were concerned with anything approaching official city planning.

At the turn of the century, these deplorable urban conditions triggered efforts to reform municipal government (Gallion, 1950). One consequence of these efforts was the establishment in 1907 of the first city planning commission, in Hartford, Connecticut, and nine years later the first zoning ordinance covering different categories of land use in New York City.

> In theory, the function of this new agency [was] to correlate the official plans prepared in the various municipal departments, to pass upon unofficial plans or suggestions for improvement, and to make plans of its own in all cases where no existing agency [had] jurisdiction. (Shurtleff, 1914)

But this has not occurred. Had the city planning commission evolved as Flavel Shurtleff indicates was intended in theory, it would be fulfilling a much needed function in municipal government today—and a book on continuous city planning would be concerned with advancing rather than inaugurating the process.

During the first half of this century, the master plans of many cities in the United States were prepared by outside consultants. Several private firms produced dozens, if not hundreds, of physical city plans concerned with major streets and highways, land use, parks, civic centers, and perhaps one or two additional spatial elements. Proposals were formulated as map-plans, distributed as part of oversize brochures or books.

> Scores of comprehensive plans were made for large and medium-sized American cities during the 1920s. In virtually every case the emphasis was on two principal elements—the major street system and zoning. (Goldfield, Brownell, 1979)

As will be discussed more fully later, such master plans were largely useless because they did not incorporate the range of political, socioeconomic, and other elements that must be considered by those governing a city and must, therefore, be part of an effective master plan.

> Occasionally an [outside consultant] may provide perspective; almost never does he have enough knowledge to advise soundly on tactical moves. (Kissinger, 1979)

These physical plans formulated by consultant firms were further flawed because they presented a concept of the city as someone from beyond its borders concluded it should be many years in the future, but without determining whether or how this could be achieved with the resources available. Or, equally likely to occur, the master plans portrayed little more than certain physical improvements and additions to existing systems that the several municipal departments concerned intended to carry out anyway. And the printed form of these plans was so expensive and inflexible that they could not be modified fast enough to take into account unexpected developments, which occur repeatedly in real life.

It is not surprising, therefore, that the master city plans of this period drawn by outside consultants were quickly relegated to the shelves of municipal libraries as evidence of money spent or as items of historical or academic interest, since they could be put to little practical use. This was also the era when the planning commission form of city planning was most energetically advocated and widely adopted. In the eyes of regular, full-time municipal officials, however, city planning commissioners were "outside consultants." Their part-time involvement in urban affairs precluded their formulating sound city plans. The idea that they would bring integrity and enlightenment to city hall rankled those responsible for governing the city and indirectly caused commissions to produce idealistic rather than workable master city plans. The fact that the commission form of city planning persists in the United States despite these limitations is another reason for turning to continuous city planning as described in this book.

RECENT DEVELOPMENTS

Early in the present century, zoning for multiple land uses was inaugurated, and it spread so steadily that few cities in the United States are without this form of land-use control today. It was presumed from the beginning that zoning would be one of the primary ways of implementing master city plans. But master plans that could be used to direct the development of cities were not produced, for reasons discussed elsewhere in this book. Zoning maps did exist, however, in response to public pressure to prevent completely incompatible land uses side by side—

such as the slaughterhouse in a residential area that gave birth to zoning. As a consequence, for many years city planning decisions and actions were based on zoning maps designating legally permissible land uses. This was a totally inadequate substitute for master plans representing broad analytical study, incorporating the primary elements of the city, and including zoning. In some cities, master plans existed on paper, but they were neither adopted officially as legal references, nor accepted as informal guides. City planning decisions were still based on zoning maps that showed land uses quite different from those shown on master plans. Only recently has the California legislature, for example, enacted a state law requiring that the zoning maps of nonchartered cities and of counties conform with their master plans. The effective date for a similar law specifically for Los Angeles has been deferred to 1982. (California Legislature, 1971–1972)

The city management movement developed at about the same time as zoning. Its aim was to improve administrative management at the topmost level of municipal government. In addition, through the years, associations of policemen, firemen, tax assessors, and other professional people have worked to improve the capabilities of their respective personnel and thereby to advance the performance of the functional activity or municipal department with which they are concerned. Both of these activities have improved city government.

The most significant actions affecting city planning during the past half century have resulted from the federal government's desire to upgrade local government and improve urban conditions. With the rapid growth in the number and size of cities in the United States, the increasing percentage of the population living in them, and the multiplication and magnification of urban problems, the federal government has necessarily become more and more involved in city planning. It can hardly abrogate its responsibilities with respect to cities, which are so socioeconomically and politically dominant in the nation today.

The federal government has applied incentives and imposed requirements at the local levels of government to achieve objectives that it believes are desirable from a national point of view and are in the best interests of the localities as well. This is achieved by offering monetary support if specified conditions are met, by setting standards that must be met before money is paid, or by threatening to cut off assistance if prescribed actions are not taken or required plans are not prepared. Since the federal government permeates almost every aspect of local life, the opportunities for monetary persuasion or sanctions are legion: grants for municipal utilities, safety and security services, public health facilities, low-cost housing, employment, social services—in fact, most government activities.

The return to local governments of a portion of the taxes collected by the federal government (revenue sharing) has been an exception to this conditional giving, but from the viewpoint of local governments it may simply substitute conditions imposed by state governments for those previously prescribed by the federal government. Revenue sharing involves only a small part of federal expenditures and disbursements, and there is talk of discontinuing this recent innovation and returning to direct federal grants and allocations.

The greatest impact on cities has resulted from national encouragement of single-family home ownership through the U.S. Federal Housing Administration (FHA), starting in 1934. By subsidizing interest rates below those charged by private mortgagers, the federal government encouraged and enabled millions of Americans to purchase single-family homes, believing that this would promote stable family life and create desirable urban environments and socioeconomic conditions.

Since these homes could only be located at the periphery of cities because of high land costs farther in, federal housing policy, coupled with governmental support of better local streets and highways, led to the spatial expansion of cities and their development into great metropolitan agglomerations of almost totally uninterrupted urban development. The far-reaching effects of this spatial expansion on cities are widely recognized: more spread-out physical form; vast increase in automobile transportation; lower average residential densities; more costly public transportation; air pollution; and the greatly reduced operational efficiency of the spatially contiguous but legally separate municipal jurisdictions that make up large metropolitan areas. The impact of these spatial consequences of national housing policy on city planning is evident.

Of course, the federal government is also involved directly with cities and their planning through federal legislation. The history of federal jurisdiction over urban activities has been one of steady expansion, for example: flood control and inland waterways (Army Corps of Engineers); national highways (Federal Highway Administration); airports and airways (Federal Aviation Administration); railroads (Amtrack); nuclear power plants (Nuclear Regulatory Commission); and environmental impact (Environmental Protection Agency).

Recent environmental legislation has the greatest potential consequences for city planning. The combination of the National Environmental Policy, Refuse, Clean Air, and Resource Recovery Acts of 1970, the Water Pollution Control, Noise Control, and Coastal Zone Management Acts of 1972, and the Safe Drinking Water Act of 1974, together with other federal legislation, provide almost limitless opportunities for federal intervention in city planning.

The experience of the American architect during this century has also affected the development of city planning. It has been estimated that less than 20 percent of construction in the United States involves the architect. Most structures are built from engineering drawings, stock plans and specifications, plans produced by contractors and developers but signed by persons licensed to approve them. By contrast, in Europe almost all construction involves the architect, who has performed as city planner as well. American architects have been understandably distressed and frustrated with this comparative devaluation of the knowledge and services they can provide. Many young persons educated in architecture have turned to related fields of endeavor or entirely different occupations. A considerable number have transferred to urban design and city planning.

This has tended to perpetuate in America the historical role of the architect/engineer as physical city planner, established during several millenia of such practice in Europe. Over the past half century, however, architecture and city planning have become separate fields and professions in the United States, requiring different education and each demanding full-time application in practice. It has been found that a person cannot perform successfully as both architect and city planner. Nowadays, each field encompasses a different body of knowledge, although there is some content in common. There are simply not enough hours in the day to cover the expanding content and practice of both fields. This is equally true for those entering city planning from other related disciplines. This evolution of city planning as a distinctive field of study and professional practice in the United States is reflected in the recent inauguration in Europe of educational programs in city planning distinct from architecture.

The number of educational programs in "urban and regional planning" in the United States has grown steadily over the years. Twenty-five years ago, there were twenty-one colleges offering professional degrees, options, or majors in city planning (Adams, 1954). In 1978, there were ten universities awarding bachelor's degrees in urban and regional planning, eighty-three awarding master's degrees, and twenty-one giving the doctor of philosophy (Hamlin, 1978). All of these academic degrees emphasize physical city planning, with much less emphasis on regional planning.

These recent historical developments are noteworthy, because they constitute growing forces toward further advancement of municipal management and city planning.

PRESENT PROBLEMS AND COMPREHENSIVE PLANNING

Coupled with these historical forces shaping city planning are the present-day problems of larger cities, which show no sign of abatement unless there is carefully planned ameliorative and preventive action.

Lack of realistic financial accounting and of continuous planning brought New York City recently to the brink of bankruptcy. Congestion continues to be a serious problem in the central areas of most cities. There are fewer and fewer affordable dwelling units for low- and middle-income families. The social stresses created by this scarcity of places to live are aggravated in parts of the United States by internal migration, and in some sections of the country by the inflow of people from foreign nations with very different languages and customs. In many countries, lack of affordable shelter has produced squatter settlements. America continues its role as a "melting pot," but there is no longer the expected "pot of gold" at the end of the American rainbow, and the stresses and strains of immigration are politically and socially explosive.

Nuclear accidents and chemical spills, together with the problems of disposing of toxic wastes that will be hazardous for many years or centuries to come, are convincing the body politic that pollution can no longer be tolerated without jeopardizing public health and safety. Because it affects everyone's daily life directly and immediately, the energy crisis is most likely to convince the American people that organized governmental planning is necessary, whether we like it or not.

"Government by crisis" exists because of our persistent refusal to face reality, to recognize the inevitable consequences of ignoring problems until they become so critical that something must be done to prevent breakdown. We have hoped that somehow they would "go away" or cure themselves. We have refused to plan deliberately for their mitigation or solution. We take spurious comfort in our claim that we have somehow managed to overcome crises in the past, and can do it again—and again. But in today's critically complex and sensitively interrelated world, postponing anticipatory or corrective action until the situation has become intolerable is no longer possible, much less acceptable. Sooner or later, reacting only to crisis is socially, politically, and governmentally disastrous—even potentially fatal in the case of nuclear and other hazardous pollution.

Because we are confronted with grave urban problems and finite municipal resources, effective city planning is essential. A procedure and an analytical mechanism must be established that will record, disclose, and analyze the current condition and potentialities of the municipality; coordinate departmental activities and plans; allocate available resources of people, time, and money among component activities; and program actions over future time that will fulfill previous commitments, mitigate or solve problems, and achieve designated objectives.

The federal government continues its efforts to promote or require comprehensive planning by cities. To date, however, the comprehensive city planning desired by the federal government as a condition for funding has been honored more in the breach than in the observance. Often, master city plans have been deliberate compromises or subterfuges tacitly agreed upon by both federal and local governments. This repeated postponing or overlooking of requirements for federal aid cannot continue forever. As previously noted, California now requires that zoning maps conform with master city plans by 1982. In time, agreement between a plan and one of its means of effectuation will be required in most cities. And "master city plans" will be more than documents of limited content largely ignored.

The federal government is also pushing the states to organize and plan their governmental activities, expecting that this will encourage them to require a higher order of planning by counties and cities. And in several ways, the federal government is moving slowly toward over-all coordination of the separate plans of its many departments and independent agencies. Nevertheless, except for the limited coordination accomplished during the annual budget review process by the Bureau of Management and Budget in the Executive Offices of the President, there is no national comprehensive planning. The many left hands of the national government do not know what the equally numerous right hands are doing (*The New York Times,* 1979). A few signs that national planning programs will eventually come about are the proposals for a national land-use plan, full employment legislation involving national economic projections, establishment of a national planning body, and most recently an energy plan and program. But the lack of legislative progress in any of these areas indicates how slowly national planning programs will be adopted in the United States, in contrast with many other nations.

Inaugurating the process and analytical simulation required for effective city planning is a first step. While this needs to be accomplished in time at the state and federal levels, as well, the city is the place to start because it is possibly less complex, more directly and immediately observable and tangible, and perhaps somewhat easier to comprehend. What is demonstrated as desirable for city planning can be applied with necessary adjustments at other levels of government, to other kinds of public planning, and to planning by private enterprise.

Finally, comprehensive planning is desirable politically in the opinion of those who believe that it supports rather than endangers the democratic political process. This question has been debated for years (Hayek, 1944; Finer, 1945). If planning is considered in its most basic sense—as a way of thinking and acting inherent in human activity—it is not political in itself. It is the way planning is applied, and the extent to which it is carried, that determine whether it is democratic or undemocratic. The planning process and analytical mechanism discussed in this book are apolitical.

WHAT IS PAST IS PROLOGUE

In summary, the effects of historical city planning on the prospects and direction of development of the field today are profound. Only recently on the time scale of historical development has city planning broadened to include conceptually more than physical/spatial considerations. "City planners" therefore are no longer mainly architects and engineers but include those with different backgrounds and professional identifications.

The Utopian strain, which has existed from the beginning as a fundamental human need, has influenced city planners throughout the centuries. It relates to the kind of master plan that has been produced in the United States in recent decades and to the ineffectiveness of city planning today. Utopian thinking increases the difficulty of incorporating the reality which is necessary for planning to be more than "a snare and a delusion."

There are basic similarities among communities throughout history, but the Industrial Revolution triggered fundamental changes in the size, nature, and functioning of cities. After a long time lag, city planning and municipal management are changing accordingly. City planning commissions introduced municipalities in the United States to community planning, but the results of this activity have been negligible because of the operational isolation of these commissions.

The future form of comprehensive city planning in the United States is foreshadowed by developments since the turn of the century: multiple-use zoning; the movement toward better public administration; the many activities of the federal government promoting comprehensive city planning; overdue environmental concern and legislation; judicial decisions requiring more realistic local planning; and expanding education and research in urban and regional planning.

Grave urban problems exacerbated by people flocking to cities in most parts of the world make urban "government by crisis" no longer feasible. Without more effective planning, cities will become increasingly explosive in every sense of the word. Surely the energy crisis in the United States beginning in the early 1970s demonstrates the dire consequences of societal failure to plan ahead. More successful comprehensive city planning is essential if a breakdown of municipal government and its disastrous consequences are to be avoided.

REFERENCES

Adams, Frederick J., *Urban Planning Education in the United States,* Cincinnati (Alfred Bettman Foundation), 1954, p. 16.

Adams, Thomas, *Outline of Town and City Planning, A Review of Past Efforts and Modern Aims,* New York (Russell Sage Foundation), 1935, pp. 72, 163.

Branch, Melville C., *Comparative Urban Design, Rare Engravings, 1830–1843,* New York (Arno), 1978, p. 95.

Branch, Melville C., "Three Graphic Reconstructions of Urban Form," *Journal of the American Institute of Planners,* Vol. XXV, No. 1, February 1959, pp. 26, 34, 40.

California Legislature, 1971–1972, Regular Session: Assembly Bill 1301, Chapter 1446 of the Government Code; 1977–1978, Assembly Bill 283, effective 1 January 1979, Amendment to Section 65860 of the Government Code (requiring zoning maps of charter cities with a population over 1,000,000—in effect, only the City of Los Angeles—to agree with their master plans); 1979–1980, Assembly Bill 1639, extends effective date of Assembly Bill 283 to 1 July 1982, approved by Governor, 23 July 1979.

Croix, Horst de la, *Military Considerations in City Planning: Fortifications,* New York (George Braziller), 1972, p. 54.

Egorov, Iurii Alekseevich (translator, Erich Dluhosch), *The Architectural Planning of St. Petersburg,* Athens, Ohio (Ohio University), 1969, pp. xx, xxvi.

Finer, Herman, *Road to Reaction,* Boston (Little, Brown), 1945, 228 pp.

Gallion, Arthur B., *The Urban Pattern,* City Planning and Design, Princeton (Van Nostrand), 1950, p. 75.

Goldfield, David R. and Brownell, Blaine A., *Urban America, From Downtown to No Town,* Boston (Houghton Mifflin), 1979, p. 362.

Hamlin, Roger E., editor, *Guide to Graduate Education in Urban and Regional Planning,* Third Edition, Chicago (American Planning Association), 1978, 401 pp.

Hammond, Lawrence (Le Breton), "The Industrial Revolution," *The Encyclopaedia Britannica,* Fourteenth Edition, Vol. 12, New York (Encyclopaedia Britannica), 1929, p. 30.

Hayek, Friedrich A., *The Road to Serfdom,* Chicago (University of Chicago), 1944, 248 pp.

Johnson, Philip, "Camera Three: Philip Johnson," Channel 28, Los Angeles, 8 November 1979, 10:00 P.M.

Kahn, Judd, *Imperial San Francisco, Politics and Planning in an American City, 1897–1906,* Lincoln, Nebraska (University of Nebraska), 1980; quoted in *Urban Studies,* University of Nebraska Press Announcement.

Kissinger, Henry, *White House Years,* Boston (Little, Brown), 1979, p. 39.

Moore, Charles, *Daniel H. Burnham, Architect, Planner of Cities,* Boston (Houghton Mifflin), 1921, Vol. II, p. 147.

Mumford, Lewis, *The City in History; Its Origins, Its Transformations, and Its Prospects,* New York (Harcourt, Brace & World), 1961, pp. 303, 360, 478, 458–474.

The New York Times Magazine, "Why Have One When Many Will Do?", 16 September 1979, pp. 114–116, 118–119.

Shurtleff, Flavel, *Carrying Out the City Plan, The Practical Application of American Law in the Execution of City Plans,* New York (Survey Associates), 1914, p. 190.

Spreiregen, Paul D., *Urban Design: The Architecture of Towns and Cities,* New York (McGraw-Hill), 1965, pp. 35, 30–32.

Part Two
THE SITUATION TODAY

The oldest communities in the United States are only about 350 years old, considerably younger than many cities in other parts of the world. During approximately 150 years of colonial existence and 200 years as an independent nation, the country has expanded from coast to coast, increased its population from about 3,000,000 to 230,000,000, become 75 percent urban, passed through its own Industrial Revolution and several technological transformations, and developed in the myriad ways reflected in the human and physical resources of the nation to be seen on all sides.

Of course, various forms of planning were required for this national achievement. Without planning, communities could not have been founded. Housing could not have been constructed; municipal utilities and services could not have been gradually provided. Canals, railroads, and the host of other public works could not have been built. Whatever the shortcomings of what has been done, the physical development and accumulation of people to be seen in the United States today is an awesome achievement in a relatively short time.

But the extent of this burgeoning and the nature of the society within which it took place made comprehensive city planning difficult, if not impossible, during a period when untrammeled growth rather than orderly development was the order of the day. The quality of municipal government and its responsibilities for reasonable directive control evolved only gradually. Urban problems today—and they are numerous and serious—are probably no worse than in the past.

> The problems of the nation's cities—pollution, crime, riots, a lack of planning, transportation—are bad, but they were worse in the proverbial "good old days. . . ." Some of the problems which dismayed the urban dweller during [the nineteenth century] are still with us—poor planning, summer riots in low-income neighborhoods, intrusion of other governments, police relations and public transportation. "Pollution was a very important problem for city government in the last century, particularly with regard to water supplies. . . . The cities of the 19th century were dirty, in many ways filthier than today. . . . There was still smallpox, and they had yellow fever, malaria, cholera and typhoid. Infant mortality was high and there were other dangers. . . ." Crime was a great concern. . . . Planning of cities and their neighborhoods was dominated by land speculators and real estate developers for profit. (*The New York Times,* 1976)

It is not surprising, therefore, that the period during which the concept of comprehensive city planning emerged began only about seventy years ago, after the political reform movements and improvements in municipal facilities brought about by technological developments at the turn of the century. The following pages of Part Two are concerned with the master city planning of this period. The objective is to disclose what this past period reveals concerning what must be done in the future if city planning is to be effective.

AN ALLEGORY OF END-STATE MASTER PLANS

The humorous and perceptive essay reproduced starting on the next page bears witness to the length of time the concept of comprehensive master city planning has been with us. The essay was written forty years ago and refers to activities undertaken previously and still continuing today.

The author was Stephen Helburn (using the pseudonym of J. C. Arbuthnot), a staff member of the U.S. National Resources Planning Board (NRPB), in the Executive Offices of President Franklin Delano Roosevelt. This federal agency and its predecessor agencies with slightly different names were the center of thought and research relating to planning in the United States, from the establishment of the National Resources Committee in 1934 to the abolishment of the NRPB by Congress in 1943. They pioneered the founding of state, regional, and local planning agencies, and produced a series of authoritative studies concerning many aspects of planning, which have not since been equaled in quality. Some of these studies are as pertinent today as they were when they were first written. Interestingly, suggestions that an agency like the NRPB should be reestablished are appearing with increasing frequency, as people realize the consequences of our inability to formulate and carry out national developmental policies and plans, as do so many other nations. (*The New York Times,* 1975; Stein, 1973)

The essay was widely appreciated within the NRPB for its humor, its poking fun at professional self-deceit, its highlighting of certain foibles and pitfalls of urban and regional planning, its rich satire, the undercurrent of deserved criticism of planners, and the supreme irony of its ending. It was also appreciated by many within the organization for the accuracy of its allegations.

It is striking how long the grand master plan concept has persisted, and how pertinent Stephen Helburn's strictures are today. Except for several specific references to New Deal days, the essay could have been written yesterday. It states the case against presumed comprehensive end-state planning in terms that are no less certain because they are stated allegorically.

Planning has been an integral part of man's cultural heritage since the earliest forms of social organization to which the word "civilization" can be applied. . . . This contention is borne out by recently discovered evidence that organized social planning existed far earlier in the history of man than had heretofore been suspected.

This new item of historical evidence is a papyrus manuscript, evidently of the time of the Pharaoh Nwab'i Ch'ow, founder of the Dew'or Dynasty which ruled Egypt from about the 13th Century B.C. until the 9th. The manuscript itself, unfortunately, was burned in the great fire that destroyed the Library at Alexandria during the Roman Invasion under Mark Antony, but I have been lucky enough to obtain a photostatic copy from a Phoenician seaman who commanded one of the Roman vessels.

The hieroglyphics are exquisitely fashioned, the language refined, and the style delicate, bespeaking a cultured gentleman of the *Twad'l* (or intellectual) class. The papyrus is watermarked "Egyptian Government—for official use only" and the characters were apparently inscribed with a pa'ka feather ("The Lifetime Quill") which was at that time extremely costly, and was available (in the government service) only to officials of the class of sn'ob or higher. There is considerable authority, therefore, for ascribing authenticity to this manuscript, and it is indeed interesting to read about early planning efforts in Egypt as written by a highly cultured sn'ob of 3300 years ago.

In the third year of the reign of the gracious and merciful Nwab'i Ch'ow it came to pass in the spring of the year that the Nile was angered and began to rise above its banks. Up the stream many peasants were drowned and many houses carried away by the dark waters, but at Cairo the city was protected by levees and the palace of the Pharaoh was surrounded by a great dike, so the court was not much concerned about this flood. One ill day, however, a palace guard rushed breathless into the palace and threw himself before the Pharaoh saying that the dike around the palace was weakening, and that it would not last many more days. So the Pharaoh had his head chopped off for being a harbinger of bad tidings, and called his Planning Board.

"Gentlemen," said the Pharaoh, "we are faced with a limited emergency. The dike outside the palace is in some danger of collapse, and I would like to have you make plans for strengthening it. Don't give me any of your landscaping on top of the dike, and don't think you can keep out the Nile by zoning the palace grounds as 'dry land.' Get to work on fundamentals. If you succeed in producing a waterproof dike (or reasonable facsimile), I will reward you well—I will even make you a permanent agency; but if you fail, I will tie you to a tree in the palace yard and have the exquisite pleasure of watching the water rise above your heads." And with these words he turned back to his lyre and his lotus brandy and a dark-complected lady from up near the Second Cataract.

So the Planning Board hired some offices with a big round conference table and began to think. "First," they cried, "we must have a Plan for Planning." "Yes," cried others, "we must provide for the necessary integration at all levels of government." So they got a map of Egypt and divided it into seven regions (seven being a sacred number) and appointed a great many consultants and draftsmen for each regional office. Then they appointed several coordinators, one for each subject, such as Land, or Water, or Public Works, and finally they appointed a Grand Coordinator to coordinate the others.

When this was done, someone cried, "Our next need is for Basic Data!" "Yes!" chorused the Board, "We will set up a committee on Basic Data!"

So a Committee on Planning Data was set up, and a great many unemployed professors were appointed to this body. Then the Committee set up several Subcommittees; Subcommittees on Deficiencies in Hydrologic Data, on the Agricultural Aspects of Flood Control, on the Social Implications of Low Dike Construction, the Institutional Barriers to Effective Flood Control, Fiscal and Monetary Problems, and Engineering.

One by one these subcommittees reported. First the engineering group brought in a report that the rip-rap on the dike had washed away, and that was why it was weakening, and that this defect could be remedied by the application of a few tons of clayey earth and rip-rap. This report was disregarded, however, because the engineers who made it had the narrow, biased viewpoint of an action agency and the report itself was not comprehensive.

The Committee on Hydrologic Data had sent out its men to query the oldest inhabitants as to the history of floods, asking such questions as, "What was the highest flood crest you remember? What year?" etc. Of course, these old gaffers had unreliable memories, so that much of the information did not click, but it was handed to the statisticians who reconciled the conflicting accounts by establishing a standard deviation. This, in turn, was multiplied by the square root of pi, and was called simply The Index.

The Committee on Social Implications reported that the dike did not provide adequate play space for the underprivileged children of Cairo; that four out of five "dike families" spent less than 20 sesterces per capita per annum for leafy, green vegetables; and that the dike formed an arbitrary social barrier between the marshdwellers and the river-boat people, intensifying and sharpening class distinction. The Subcommittee recommended a sweeping investigation of relief administration and advocated the exportation of aliens living on public funds.

All this time the angry Nile was rising higher and higher. The police teletypes were flashing the latest developments: "Flood crest now 35 feet at Cairo signed O'Malley." "Water at Memphis over levees stop city water supply threatened many families stranded stop inform red cross signed Brown." The Pharaoh sent an interoffice memorandum to the Planning Board calling their attention to the fact that the emergency was less and less limited all the time, and reminding them of the dire punishment attendant upon their failure. The Board, however, refused to rush into action unprepared. "If a thing is worth doing," its Chairman wrote in the Egyptian Planning Quarterly, "It is worth doing well." And they waited for the reports of the other Committees.

The Fiscal and Monetary group said that one reason for the weakness of the dike was that it was burdened with an excessive capitalization and struggling to carry too large a debt. The dike was also, it turned out, in the jurisdiction of several layers of government all of which would have had power to tax it, if it had not been government property and therefore tax free. The Subcommittee recommended a drastic overhauling of "our antiquated tax system, the elimination of obsolete units of government, the immediate refunding of the Cairo Dike Commission's bonded obligations, and the balancing of the national budget next year."

The Committees on Agriculture and Institutional Barriers also reported but their reports were confidential, so that little is known of their findings and recommendations. It was rumored about Cairo, however, that the Agriculture group contemplated some daring experiments with a new plant called the soy bean.

During all this the Nile's waters were rising, and by the time the Board had received all its Basic Data, the water was only a few inches below the top of the big dike around the palace. The Pharaoh moved his lyre and his lotus brandy to the second floor, and sent his lady-friend to her aunt's house in a skiff. The Planning Board sent him an Interim Progress Report stressing the need for a comprehensive approach to the problem and co-ordinated effort at all levels of government. The Pharaoh sent back the report with the notation that there were only two levels of government in

Egypt, both very low, and that if they got below water level the Planning Board would go down with them.

The next step of the Planning Board was to prepare a Master Plan. The Master Plan provided for the comprehensive and integrated development of the Nile all the way from Lake Tsana to its delta—it was a social and economic as well as a physical program, designed to promote the wise conservation and utilization of all Egypt's resources, human and natural. Planning circles were inspired by the grandeur of its scope, and by the sweeping way in which broad principles and objectives were blocked out with a bold hand. The Plan called for a unified system of locks and dams to promote navigation, irrigation systems for the marshlands along the banks, and for a scenic highway along each bank from the source to the mouth. At the last minute one of the narrow-minded Engineers insisted that the plan contain some provision for strengthening the dike at Cairo, but he was regarded as an old batty, and the Board told him that this was merely a detail which could be filled in later.

When the Master Plan was completed, the Board said, "Now we must achieve decentralization of planning. This plan must not be imposed from above; it must proceed from the ground up." So a great campaign was started to have the Plan proceed from the ground up. The expensive regional consultants went around to Kiwanis meetings and D.A.R. flagwavings, and told them that Good Planning is Good Business. Boy Scouts were sent from door to door with petitions, and the Egyptian Legion paraded through the streets drumming up local demand for "The Master Plan."

Meanwhile the Plan was worked over by the Planning Board's Division of Deletion, which carefully emasculated all proposals that might rouse the antagonism of the Upstream Business Men's Association or the Nile Valley Real Estate Conference. The Plan was then printed up in tentative form and circulated for "technical review and comment" to leading scholars and public officials of the country.

All this routine was very boring to the Board, of course, since its outcome could not possibly affect the Board's decisions, so they decided to take a vacation trip on a steamer up the Nile. This was known as "checking up on the regional offices." They chartered a steamer and some private secretaries, and off they went, up the angry Nile.

Everybody said they were crazy, to go out on a boat when the Nile was in flood, and the Pharaoh sent them another memorandum reminding them that a little water was already slopping over the dike and that the puddles were knee-deep in the Palace Yard. But they said, "There is no use in devising hasty plans and attempting to evade the operation of certain Immutable Planning Laws. Half a plan is worse than none. We must not let a profusion of trees obscure our vision of the woods." So they left the regional officers in charge of integrating anything that came up, and then boarded the steamer.

The day after they left the dike gave way, and the water poured over the city of Cairo and into the Palace. Everything was washed away including the Master Plan, and everybody was drowned including the Pharaoh—everybody except the planners. When they came back they ransacked the flotsam until they found some pencils, and they sat down to drift a broader, better-coordinated Master Plan for a broader, better-coordinated Society. (Note 1)

TRADITIONAL MASTER CITY PLANS IN THE UNITED STATES: FALLACIES AND INADEQUACIES

The historical forces and events noted in Part One account for the fallacies and inadequacies of city planning in the United States satirized so aptly by Stephen Helburn in his brief allegory. What may be called the "seven deadly sins" of the end-state master plans that have characterized planning in the past 50 years or more are described and explained on the following pages in the order of their significance in preventing effective city planning.

1. *The picture of the physical city 20–25 years in the future shown by traditional end-state master plans does not represent what the community wants nor what is possible, but what city planners wish could be.*

This concept of an "end-state" plan presumes that the ultimate state of what is being planned can be correctly and conclusively conceived many years in advance of its intended realization (Figure 1). In city planning, this implies that the conditions, needs, and objectives of a living organism as complex as a city can be identified, analyzed, and projected many years into the future. It assumes that some city planner or group of individuals has the vast knowledge and technical capability to (1) select and analyze all significant elements of the city; (2) identify and quantify their multitudinous interactions; (3) project these elements and interactions in concert into the distant future; and (4) finally decide what the

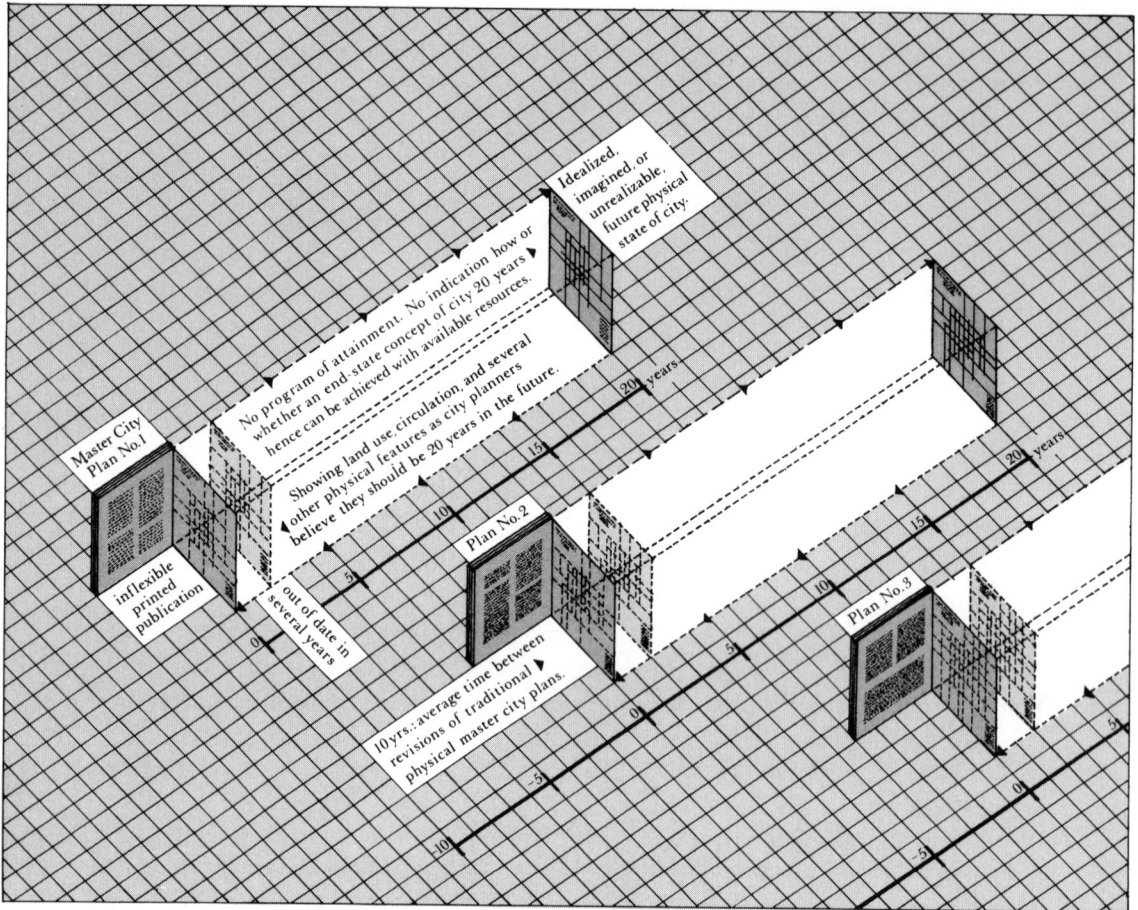

Figure 1 Schematic representation of traditional end-state master city plans.

city should be like at this future time. Unless all elements are identified and analyzed correctly, the master plan does not portray a complete and final end-state prescribed for the city, but an incomplete and tentative formulation that is a different kind of plan.

Even end-state plans for a building or engineering structure are normally subject to many minor and several major changes before the project is finished, despite the fact that the working drawings and specifications simulate the end product as completely as possible before construction begins. It is impossible to foresee all requirements and anticipate all contingencies except perhaps for the simplest activities. Certainly, the knowledge does not now exist to analyze completely organisms as complex as a city.

> Superior Judge David A. Thomas summed up what's wrong with land-use planning in Los Angeles County when he voided the county's first general plan. Thomas ruled that the environmental impact report (EIR) on which the plan was based consisted of "no more than a sterile declaration of unsupported generalities almost entirely failing to convey any factual information ... almost the entire EIR consists largely of pretentious statements of the obvious ..." in preparation for nearly a decade ... the plan was supposed to serve as a 20-year guide for granting of zoning ordinances and building permits, and the setting of important density requirements. (*Los Angeles Times*, 1975)

The organizations to which comprehensive planning is applied, including cities, and the environments within which they function always involve indefinite, undeterminable, inconsistent, and irrational human behavior, and unpredictable and catastrophic events in the physical world. "Accidents" are normal expectations rather than random exceptions to the rule in comprehensive planning. There are no absolutes; there is only a maze of interrelated and conditional probabilities. This indeterminacy precludes complete comprehension and limits what can and should be attempted. It is why flexibility is such a crucial characteristic of sound comprehensive planning.

The end-state concept presupposes that no unexpected external events or internal developments will occur that will make it imperative or desirable to revise the plan repeatedly. It assumes that the municipality is independent and self-sufficient enough to forecast and act with finality on its own long-range future, either apart from metropolitan, regional, state, federal, and international influences and events, or according to reliable projections of the future development and behavior of these entities.

This kind of master plan is therefore inflexible by definition because it does not take into account the unanticipated economic, political, social, legal, technological, and other developments which undoubtedly will occur during the twenty to twenty-five years before the plan is supposed to be realized. These developments will vitally affect the city and require revision of the plan. They may occur within the city, in its surroundings, elsewhere in the nation, or, as international interconnections become more numerous and determinative, in some far-off part of the world. To deny that unexpected changes will occur is totally unrealistic. To ignore their effects on the city and its planning is impossible. As the Greek philosopher Heraclitus noted 2500 years ago, "There is nothing permanent except change."

The end-state concept also assumes that people's desires, objectives, and priorities are sufficiently determinable and unchanging to permit drawing conclusions today with certainty concerning what they will want or accept a quarter of a century hence. Or it assumes that city planners are wise enough to anticipate public desires and intentions, and that this professional determination will be substituted for political resolution. Some people believe that a predetermined urban end state can be achieved by autocratic regimes, despite historical experience to the contrary and despite the illogic of presuming that dictatorial regimes have the required total knowledge but democratic societies do not. Such a belief requires the assumption that repressive government somehow eliminates the inevitability of change.

Perhaps city planners recognized years ago that end-state city plans were illusory but concluded nonetheless that they were the only kind that could be formally proposed to the municipal government. And any master plan was better than none. Also, local legislatures, mayors, city managers, and municipal departments have not favored city planning, despite the serious problems that have beset cities throughout history. Therefore, neither the incentives nor the governmental mechanism to conduct effective city planning have existed in the past. Because municipal utility and service systems were technologically simpler and fewer in number in the past, it may also have been concluded that they did not warrant the level of functional planning required for cities to operate nowadays.

> [The city council president] was referring to urban development plans, some of which are sponsored by the United Nations and other international agencies and call for the creation of cities within cities and green areas as a partial solution to the urban crisis. A few thousand homes have been built. But as with urban plans all over the world, they have remained largely on paper. (Vidal, 1977)

The prevalence of the end-state concept may also relate to the tendency of institutions, including cities, to "follow the leader," to take the path of least resistance or trouble. It is more difficult to introduce something new and different. It is much easier to copy than to devise or revise. Should one even question whether the master plan of another city is sound or capable of basic improvement? Does it really matter, when master city plans in the United States so often fulfill the superficial purpose of displaying concern for the future, rather than serving as a significant instrument of municipal management and city planning? It is surprising how often bureaucracies pick the path of least resistance by simply adopting without critical review the conclusions and procedures of similar institutions. Often, this means adopting features that are not appropriate for the new application, or incorporating actual mistakes that were made in the original and never corrected.

> During the late 15th and entire 16th centuries, a number of popes worked to achieve an urban design for the entire city comprising a system of straight avenues: linking the seven great pilgrimmage churches of Rome, providing impressive vistas expressive of the power and glory of the Church, attaining a spatial aesthetic unity, and facilitating the movement of traffic between different parts of the city during this period. (Branch, 1978)

Belief in the idea of end-state city plans was more understandable in times past. Royal or other absolute authority could sometimes effect extensive changes in the physical city in a short time, and approval by the population at large was rarely considered and even more rarely required. But changed circumstances affected royal plans as they do all plans. And even if the form of the city visualized in the end-state plan was beyond attainment, it provided the aesthetic satisfaction of any imaginary concept that might be realized by some subsequent ruler.

2. *Physical plans do not treat financial, economic, political, social, technological, and other "nonphysical" realities which must be incorporated in meaningful city plans.*

It is a conclusion of the city planning profession itself that the limitation of this activity in the past to a few physical elements and rather superficial urban analysis has been at least partly responsible for its insignificance in the United States. It has become increasingly clear throughout the years that economic and financial factors are involved in every aspect of city planning. For example, tax policies are as important as zoning in the determination of urban land use. Our laws and institutions define the method and extent of urban planning. The respective roles of government and private enterprise are continually evolving. New technologies introduce improved ways of doing things, creating problems as well as opportunities. How city planning in the United States could intellectually justify its partial approach in the past seems almost incomprehensible now. But other fields review their past with the same disbelief which comes with added knowledge and changing concepts. As indicated in the introduction to this book, "comprehensive" is the adjective used to denote the broadened concept of city planning today.

Cities are first and foremost economic organisms, although historical circumstances may blur this persistent fact during times when military, religious, governmental, or other shaping forces predominate. If economic activities were not responsible for the founding of the city and the selection of its site in the first place, they determine how long the city will survive and grow, and how much external trade, economic support, or subsidy in one form or another will be required.

Therefore, master city plans are neither valid nor useful if they do not treat the economic base of the city, whether it be the production or processing of natural resources, manufacturing trade, commerce, service and supply, government, transportation, recreation, another economic activity, or a combination of several of these. This productive base identifies the activities that not only support the city's economy but represent at the same time its vulnerability to changes within and outside the city that affect its economic health.

The economic situation and prospects of the city determine its capacity to provide public services, planned improvements, and urban redevelopment. They relate to the type of people living in the city and their incomes, the financial rating and ability of the city to borrow money, the social and political situations created by unemployment, available cultural facilities, and most other aspects of the community.

The most obvious sin of omission in present city plans is that they bear no relation to the economic and fiscal capabilities of the community. The municipal budget is ignored as are forecasts of tax revenues and other income, grants and indirect financial support, and the projected future expenditures required to maintain and improve public facilities and services. The operating plans of the municipal departments, calling for expenditures programmed over a period of years, are not incorporated or taken into account. (Note 2)

Economic and financial realities are simply not considered. It is conveniently assumed that whatever economic conditions and financing are required will come about somehow or be provided in some way. With such omissions and mistaken assumptions, end-state master plans are little more than pipedreams.

Since the modern era of city planning in the United States was partly a response to gross municipal inefficiency and corruption in local government, city planning commissions were established as recommendatory bodies to help bring honesty and greater representation of the public interest to city hall. Ever since, city planning has tended to divorce itself from politics and regular municipal administration, analytically as well as operationally. City planning makes its recommendations to the legislative body of the municipality, which makes the final decisions in the form of laws and other legislative action. The mayor or city manager has a role in the city planning process, its nature and importance depending on the provisions of the municipal charter and the political situation. Certainly, in the city of Chicago during the middle of this century, all city planning and every other activity of local government required the approval of Richard Daley during his long tenure as mayor and political arbiter. On the other hand, in many communities the mayor performs a largely ceremonial role and the legislature is preeminent.

The physical/spatial content of most city plans ignores politics. It is assumed that political decision-makers and the body politic will find these formulations desirable and attainable. City plans have not, therefore, reflected political realities, nor have they incorporated recommendations responding constructively to the political requirements for effective city planning, despite the fact that city planners recognize politics as the major force determining the intent and content of city planning. They see their end-state master plans ignored, rejected, or radically revised without hesitation by the political decision-makers of the municipality.

The pervasive significance of politics has, of course, been demonstrated throughout history. As the "science and art of government . . . the theory or practice of managing affairs of public policy or of political parties . . .", politics has permeated human affairs since earliest times. While it is a way of gradually reconciling differences among people and advancing their collective condition, politics embodies self-centered and parochial interests. It involves emotional, volatile, and conflictive forces rather than consensus, rationality, and scientific analysis, which are emphasized in planning. Resolving political differences usually takes a prolonged period of time, with many trials and tribulations in the accomplishment. Most elected politicians avoid comprehensve planning because they believe that it interferes with the practical requirements for reelection. Furthermore, someone else will get the credit for effective planning if its benefits are to be noted only at some future time.

> Presidents [of the United States] are generally suspicious of long-range planning and overly-fixed views. . . . Pass now, plan later. . . . The difficulty of long-range planning: In addition to being hard to do, setting long-term goals can be politically embarrassing, if not dangerous, for a president. It forces him to run the risk of being prematurely judged by what he has yet to accomplish. (Barron, 1975)

> Congress characteristically shies away from the subject of planning when too plainly labeled as such. Congress is tied to the single-year appropriations cycle by habit and organization. Federal agencies are accustomed to the short budget cycle and suspicious of longer term planning because it implies a central planning authority interposed between them and the budget.

> Congress also unquestionably is influenced by an uncomfortable feeling that government planning goes against the American grain. Talk of the planned society or planned economy stirs visions of the tolalitarian state. Even without the authoritarian connotations, there is a conviction that circumstakes change and planners make mistakes. . . .

> Perhaps most important are the practical difficulties of planning in this country's [United States] proverbially pluralistic system. (Walsh, 1980)

> Legislators, and particularly legislative leaders, tend by the very nature of their job . . . to react rather than initiate, focus on one issue at a time rather than an overall program. They push popular positions rather than unpopular ones, try to work out quiet compromises rather than to shape and lead opinion. . . . The legislative leader rarely focuses on a broad, long-range program. He's always working on the bill coming to the floor tomorrow, getting his troops in line and working out the compromises and deals to pick up missing votes. He's rarely too concerned about the way the bill might or might not fit in with a dozen others in the legislative pipeline. . . .

> The legislator operates in a very short frame of reference. He doesn't plan. (Otten, 1974)

> Why should a Mayor go through with the agony of change which he can only start, when his successor is going to get the benefit and the credit later, because that's when it will be noticeable? (Cowan, 1972)

Also, the problems continuously presented to politicians by their constituencies have to do with the here and now, almost to the exclusion of tomorrow, much less of the longer-range future. These immediate demands leave politicians with little time to consider general policies for the future. Data collection, analysis, planning, and effectuation are relegated to the government bureaucracy. In many different ways, politics either within the municipality or within its external environment determines the form, content, and means of accomplishing comprehensive city planning.

City planners have avoided direct treatment and statement of political realities in their end-state plans, which have been severely limited in their coverage and their specific recommendations, to avoid being politically challenged and rejected. The content of present-day master city plans implicitly disclaims politics as an unwanted restriction on the capability of staff planners to formulate what ought to be; ignores politics as too difficult to handle, as parochial, or corrupt; or allows politics to limit city planning proposals excessively. The political process and the politician are not involved directly in the formulation of the plans that they are asked by city planners to approve and implement.

As cities grow, social factors become more critical. They are, of course, important in small communities where contacts between socially different individuals and small groups are close and frequent. In large cities, socially different groups are communities in themselves, occupying separate sections of the city which are characterized by different public facilities, services, amenities, levels of danger to persons and damage to property, and physical deterioration.

These differences, together with the greater potential for disruption inherent in situations where large numbers of people have common causes and complaints, make social conditions an essential consideration in city planning—as much to avoid unrest as to improve the lot of the less fortunate. Throughout the history of the United States, formulating social policies and plans has been made especially difficult by the waves of internal migration and of immigration from foreign lands that have occurred repeatedly and continue today. America is certainly one of the most ethnically diverse nations on earth.

City planning in the United States has always favored decent dwelling units for low-income people, provided by publicly financed housing if not by private enterprise. As noted in Part One of this book, the establishment of city planning commissions around the turn of the last century was associated with better housing for the poor as part of municipal government reform. City planners' hearts, however, have always been more socially responsive than their professional recommendations. Housing has finally been added recently as a required element of official city plans in California, but there is confusion and difference of opinion concerning what information, analytical conclusions, and proposed actions will best meet this requirement.

There is a growing awareness of social considerations in city planning, brought about by severe social situations in the central areas of many cities and the frightening urban disturbances of the late 1960s. Researchers are seeking reliable "social indicators" that will indicate the social conditions of the city and its subareas at any time, and show whether aggregate social improvements are being made over time. It is hoped that, in addition, such indicators may give advance warning of potentially explosive social situations. (Sheldon, Parke, 1975)

Despite this history of concern, city planning in the United States has not strongly and consistently advocated low-cost housing, formulated a set of policies directed to improving the condition of the urban poor, nor recommended other social actions—much less indicated how such social improvements could be progressively accomplished. For example, desegregation is an established public policy, but it is rarely explicitly reflected in city plans. As is the case with the economic and political elements, a social element has not been formulated and incorporated into end-state municipal master plans.

Of the many technological advances of the past century and a half, the automobile has certainly had the most profound and far-reachng effects on cities in industrialized nations. The urban consequences of this technological advance are the only ones which are included in physical city plans. Primary highway networks, secondary street systems, and subdivision designs have been primary concerns of city planning for many years and are shown on all master city plans. But planning and implementing the urban transportation system and other technological systems with pervasive impacts on cities is not done by city planning departments. This planning is done by other municipal departments, government agencies, or private enterprises with functional responsibility for one or several urban elements involving sophisticated technology: water supply, energy production, waste disposal, electronic communication, construction, rail and air transportation.

Public utilities support what has been aptly called the "metabolism of cities" (Wolman, 1965), that is to say, the life system of supply and disposal that sustains the city's population and enables it to function as a viable urban organism and environment. Without utility systems to supply water and energy to the urban body, to dispose of its waste, and to provide communication, the modern city could not function and would revert to a more primitive state. Urban inhabitants often forget their extreme vulnerability, their dependence on "someone else" to provide them with the absolute necessities of life once provided by the family unit.

As previously noted in another connection, the operating and long-range plans of municipal departments, governmental bodies, and private enterprises in the city—including those responsible for technological operations—are not reviewed and coordinated as part of the city planning process. Besides sustaining human life in the industrialized city, technological elements determine the city's physical form, as seen from high above. The primary "organs" of the urban anatomy—industrial, commercial, and residential structures—are located where they can be connected with the skeletal systems of utility lines and other urban services that enable communities to function. Yet the widespread and increasing impacts of science and technology on cities are at best indirectly reflected in traditional master city plans.

3.   *Traditional city plans are formulated as if the municipal government can provide whatever funds are needed and will enact whatever laws and regulations are required to achieve the end-state city planners believe is desirable many years hence.*

People must want or be willing to commit themselves a quarter of a century in advance to specific objectives, standards, priorities, and expenditures for public services, education, transportation, land use, housing, business, industry, recreation, and other elements of the future city. Very few democratic societies will do this, since it requires not only resolving many basic issues and questions that are nowhere near settled, but committing specific resources to these undecided ends.

People are unwilling to forego more than a few of the services and satisfactions provided by the current use of available resources in favor of their use and enjoyment by other people at some future time. In the past, religious beliefs provided a motivation for such sacrifice. Forebearance today would produce rewards in the afterlife. This no longer applies to the same extent. The desire of have-nots for what others possess is vastly increased by the instant information supplied to almost everyone today by the mass media; and they want to acquire these possessions or privileges immediately. They believe that government should apply all available resources to this end.

Many questions would have to be answered before a true end-state master plan could be formulated. Will the form of the end-state city be compact and dense in the distant future, or dispersed with low density? The answer to this question depends on the development of energy sources and public choices concerning the use of energy. How is the developmental effort to be divided between limited-access highways and rail transit, between open space and built-up land, or between pollution control and industrial production? Can desired developmental goals be effected without jeopardizing the economc health of the city?

Since there is never enough money to meet all needs and desires, how are financial resources and the facilities they pay for to be allocated? For example, between correctional and preventive law-enforcement and fire-protection facilities; hospitals and neighborhood health-maintenance clinics; general and commercial aviation; or between parks, playgrounds, and public open space on the one hand, and land covered with structures producing private income and municipal taxes?

The answers to such broad but basic questions determine the form, facilities, and functioning of the future city. What changes, if any, in education are to be provided for and reflected in the budget, physical installations, culture, and human resources of the end-state city? Can the steadily increasing per capita demands for water, energy, waste disposal, and telecommunications be met? What standards are to be attained by the time of realization of the end-state plan in twenty to twenty-five years, with respect to environmental pollution of the air, water, and ground by chemicals, biologicals, radiation, and noise? How will dwelling units be divided among highrise structures, row and cluster housing, and detached single-family homes?

What changes, if any, are likely to be made in present land-use controls? Will land ownership, the urban real estate market, and urban development remain essentially the same as they are today? Should today's taxes, their type and percentage of family income, be extrapolated to determine future municipal income? Will there be changes in the form and extent of financial support provided to municipalities by higher levels of government? Will cities encourage particular kinds of development by direct or indirect subsidies and incentives, or, like many European cities, will they engage in the kind of land development now left entirely to private enterprise in the United States? Is the spatial dispersal of minority and low-income groups to be finally effected in the end-state urban condition? Are provisions for civilian defense in the event of war to be incorporated into the physical city, as they are in Switzerland, Sweden, the Soviet Union, Israel, and China?

These illustrative questions are of much more than speculative or theoretical interest; answers are required before the end-state of a city at some distant future time can be conceived. To be sure, every single question and relevant detail need not be answered today. But logically as well as practically, a future end-state for a city cannot be conceived without assumptions or conclusions concerning the characteristics of the primary elements of which it is composed, their interrelationships, underlying forces and attitudes that determine what is likely to occur, what can and will be accomplished in the way of advancement, and specific means and mechanisms of effectuation. Without this prior determination, the end-state concept of a master city plan is a fantasy or a deception. For the foreseeable future, such prior determination is neither analytically possible nor politically forthcoming.

Adoption of an end-state city plan would require that the body politic or its representatives accept its illusory premises. Besides the electorate being unwilling to commit extensive resources to an indefinite and distant future, people are far too discerning *collectively* to believe the false premises of the grand master plan concept discussed above. These premises violate the common sense that people apply so effectively to unrealistic claims and aspirations by their governments. In autocratic societies, the populace cannot express active disagreement or opposition, but in their own minds people are as skeptical of what they know to be unrealistic or otherwise unattainable as those living in freer societies.

> The intensive period of structure *plan-making* during the first two-thirds of the 1970s served in some ways to deflect planners' attention away from planning as a continuous process. Perhaps because it had to be formally submitted to central government there was a tendency to think of the structure plan as an end-state plan. One important consequence was that monitoring activity tended to be ignored until the plan was submitted. (Batey, Breheny, 1978)

Even if elected representatives or appointed officials delude themselves into thinking that long-range end-state master plans are really attainable—or desirable for other reasons even if unattainable—the populace knows better. They recognize that both the genuine effort and the pretense will fail because of the inherent fallacies in the concept, not because their wishes receive little attention in such planning.

> When self-interest is involved, public opinion in a democracy is likely ahead of official policy. . . . By and large, if people in a democracy are provided educational opportunities and ready access to information, public opinion reveals a hard-headed common sense. The more enlightened people are to the implications of events and proposals for their own self-interest, the more likely they are to agree with the more objective opinions of realistic experts. (Cantril, 1944)

4.   The end-state depicted in city plans is so far in the future and so idealized that it does not represent the outcome of a feasible sequence of shorter-range municipal operations and attainments.

A corollary of traditional city planning has been strong emphasis on the general and the long-range future, and minimization of the specific and near-term. It was presumed that after commitment to an end-state master plan, the city planning commission and department or the municipal operating departments could develop the strategies, tactics, funds, mechanisms, programs, and schedules required for its attainment. This has not worked out because this determination of how the plan can be implemented, rather than being secondary, is the essence of real planning and the most difficult part of the process. To prepare plans without reference to their effectuation and to restrictive urban realities is relatively easy. Resources can be presumed to exist which in fact are not available. Instruments of effectuation can be assumed to exist that may be a long time coming and may never be provided. Positive outcomes can be presupposed for crucial socioeconomic, political, legal, and procedural questions that in fact are still strongly debated and far from consensus.

Some people maintain that the longer-range aspects of planning can be determined apart from the specifics of short-range activities. They differentiate between "strategic" planning, which is concerned with policies, objectives, and general plans for ten to twenty years hence, and "operational" planning, which requires precise plans and programs to direct manufacturing, processing, servicing, or any other ongoing current activity.

> Master Plans cannot be a substitute for having as a permanent part of the machinery of government a planning process through which data on

the condition of the Metropolitan Area are kept current and through which policies, long-range plans and specific action programs are evolved continually in response to current needs. (Karachi Development Authority, 1974)

Usually, strategic plans need to be reviewed only every few years, or when some event calls for immediate reconsideration. Operating plans normally need change or adjustment quarterly, monthly, weekly, daily, or even hourly, depending on the activity. And processes such as oil refining, electric power generation, and war require continuous monitoring of operations (real-time monitoring).

Separation of strategic and operational planning presumes that current plans and decisions do not significantly affect long-range objectives, policies, and plans. Supposedly, short-range variations will average out and have no effect on the long-range plan: strategic plans will retain their usefulness and validity despite considerable change in operating plans.

There is no such distinction in actuality. All elements and aspects of an organism function interdependently, continuously, and progressively over time. Every internal event, decision, or plan today affects the immediate, intermediate, and long-range future of the organism in some way. The effect may be remote and inconsequential. It may be difficult or impossible to specify because it is so subtle. Information may not be available to determine cause and effect. Or the functioning of the organism may not be well enough understood to trace and calculate the consequences.

> It has become almost axiomatic that, to the extent you consider more elements as variable, you multiply the number of possible outcomes and thereby shorten the practical planning cycle. (Lamson, 1975)

We know from experience that seemingly minor occurrences can have both immediate effects and long-range and far-reaching outcomes, and as pointed out by Benjamin Franklin long ago:

> A little neglect may breed mischief; for want of a nail the shoe was lost; for want of a shoe the horse was lost; and for want of a horse the rider was lost.

Neglecting presumably minor elements or events in planning can produce a magnified effect on a crucial component of the organism, or a small effect with pervasive and cumulative repercussions. In civil government, for example, an action changing an environmental standard may affect the cost and benefit of the public service involved for years. In business, a change in the interest rate determines the cost of borrowing needed capital, and change in the rate of payment by customers (receivables) affects cash flow, which in turn affects the financial condition of the enterprise and its future. In war, a shift in enemy strategy or tactics causes immediate compensating adjustments, which are reflected throughout the military establishment.

Were it possible for the current performance of an organism to continue exactly as it has in the past or precisely as projected, strategic plans could be fixed for the longer-range future. But all organizations are subject to the impact of external events and internal conditions that were not or could not be anticipated. Witness the widespread effects of the severe reduction in property taxes brought about by Proposition 13 in California. When such an unanticipated event occurs, the organism is affected adversely if operations and plans are not revised immediately. For this reason, short-range and long-range plans cannot be formulated separately. Goals, policies, and plans can be developed for the long-range future, but if they are to remain unchanged, they must be so general that they are aspirations or statements of intent rather than plans and programs to attain specific objectives. If long-range plans are specific, they are *ipso facto* invalidated by the frequent changes made necessary by unexpected events and changes of objective.

End-state master city plans can be drawn only because they do *not* consider municipal operations and current events. They ignore existing urban obligations which cannot be discontinued, such as the time and money committed to public safety, utilities, education, pensions, and various municipal services. They do not take into account the resources required to provide growing urban populations with these same services. They do not incorporate the limits on available manpower and funds set by the size and composition of the population, the local economy, and the natural resources of the city. The functioning city and the idealized city are considered separate and distinct in end-state plans.

Long-range comprehensive plans commonly reveal a desired state of affairs. They rarely specify the detailed courses of action needed to achieve the desired state. By their long-run nature they cannot do so. The development plan, in contrast, will indicate the specific changes in land use programmed for each year, the rate of new growth, the public utilities to be built, the structures to be removed, the private investment required, the

extent and sources of public funds to be raised, the tax and other local incentives to encourage private behavior requisite to the plan. (Meyerson,
1956)

In the real world, a long-range idealized version of a city cannot be effected apart from the existing community. Realistic planning must evolve
from the city as it exists in fact except in the special case of a new town
built in open country. Urban development is limited by the finite resources available which must not only provide for the continued functioning of the city, but also support its gradual improvement. The
manpower and money required for any organism to continue functioning
as it has in the past cannot suddenly be reduced without causing severe
economic disruption with serious social and political consequences.
Were operating funds to be withdrawn entirely, the city of course could
not survive. Changes are also limited chronologically by the lead times
required to complete new construction and to attain any desired objective, and by the successive steps involved in performing any endeavor.

Another mistaken assumption of the end-state concept is that master
plans can be broadly "general" and need not deal with "details," which
should be handled by those engaged in "operations" rather than by
those concerned with "master planning." Certainly, there are long-range
strategic planning policies that are general in nature and essential to the
effective conduct of most organizations and activities. Examples are the
crucial strategic planning decision by the United States during World
War II to win in Europe before turning to Japan and the Pacific, and the
decision of a business corporation to plan years ahead to manufacture
and sell its products abroad. But such long-range strategic policies and
plans are practically useless unless their possible realization is determined by precise examination of shorter-range operating conditions and
plans. The decision to concentrate first on victory in the European the-
ater of war depended on detailed examination of operational logistics,
tactical forces and plans, and other military considerations, which revealed that the United States could not wage war successfully on two extensive and widely separated military fronts at the same time. Nor can a
business corporation sensibly plan a strategic expansion abroad until it
determines that it has the operating capability to do so by examining its
competitive position, financial reserves and prospective profitability, the
market for its products in Europe, the availability of the necessary labor
force and management personnel, and many other vital details. The success of a long-range plan may depend on what end-state planners would

consider a detail: a city plan on a tax rate or a particular political decision, a corporate plan on the cost of a critical material or a specific government regulation.

Not only must the planning process continue without interruption, as we shall see, but it must treat short- and long-range plans as part of an analytic continuum, which may reveal that an operating detail today shapes the long-range plans, and a long-range strategic policy determines certain features of operating plans. Successful city planning requires coincident consideration of the general and the specific, strategy and tactics, short-range and long-range, present and ultimate. When master plans are conceptually and analytically isolated from current conditions, activities, and operating plans, they are useless for their intended purpose. At best, they may serve to establish general goals rather than planning objectives (Branch, Robinson, 1968).

> The first thing to do to make sure that a program will not have results is to have a lofty objective—"health care," for instance, or "to aid the disadvantaged." Such sentiments belong in the preamble. They explain why a specific program or agency is being initiated rather than what the program is meant to accomplish. . . . To use such statements as "objectives" thus makes sure that no effective work will be done. For work is always specific, always mundane; always focused. Yet without work there is non-performance.
>
> To have a chance at performance, a program needs clear targets, the attainment of which can be measured, appraised, and at least judged. (Drucker, 1980)

5. *City planning has attempted to function independently of politics and separately from the administrative processes of the municipality.*

Because of the conceptual and analytical separation of long- and short-range plans just discussed, city planning in the United States has had little relationship to the operating units of municipal government concerned with the protection of persons and property, building and safety, public works, public utilities, traffic and transportation, health, social services, recreation and parks, libraries, budget and finance, or data services. How planning a municipality actually occurs, and the relatively minor role of traditional city planning, is shown in Figure 2, which is based on the situation in Los Angeles, California.

Local planning should be given or must gain for itself a place in the structure of government, where it will be closer to the local legislative body, the chief executive, and administrative departments. (U.S. National Resources Committee, 1937)

If it is to be functional and practical in nature, planning must consider the needs of the line departments and the realities of municipal finance.

Planning calls for combined efforts in public administration at the municipal level. The master plan will not live and develop if it is only the brain child of a planning commission. It can become a beautiful book of maps and projects, without any real impact on the community. For implementation, legal action by the council must be forthcoming. . . . The council, as well as the planning commission, must be in support of the master plan. If the council frequently overrules the planners, comprehensive planning becomes an ineffective art. During any administration, much will depend on the support which the chief executive gives the master plan. . . . The line departments . . . must understand the comprehensive plan and work forward to its objectives. (Bromage, 1957)

We need to plan for every function of government—education, police, fire, health and garbage collection. Planning is not limited to community development or master plans. . . . In some cases, planning remains so independent it may be isolated and therefore ineffective. To be effective, planning must be integrated into all functions and levels of governments. (Lieder, 1977)

Municipal general managers and administrative heads are responsible for a functional area of activity. Because they are necessarily concerned with current problems, existing conditions, and the limited resources available, they regard "master planners" as idealistic and unrealistic, their proposed master city plans of little use because of the typical limitations. Addressing themselves almost exclusively to land use, most master plans do not incorporate the operating plans of municipal departments, although some physical facilities programmed for the future by departments may appear in the land-use plans. These are almost totally unrelated to the urban realities which operating officials must cope with continually. Nor do they include actions directed toward resolving the most vital, difficult, and controversial issues confronting the city. The city administrative officer of one large city in the United States has gone so far as to call such master plans a fraud.

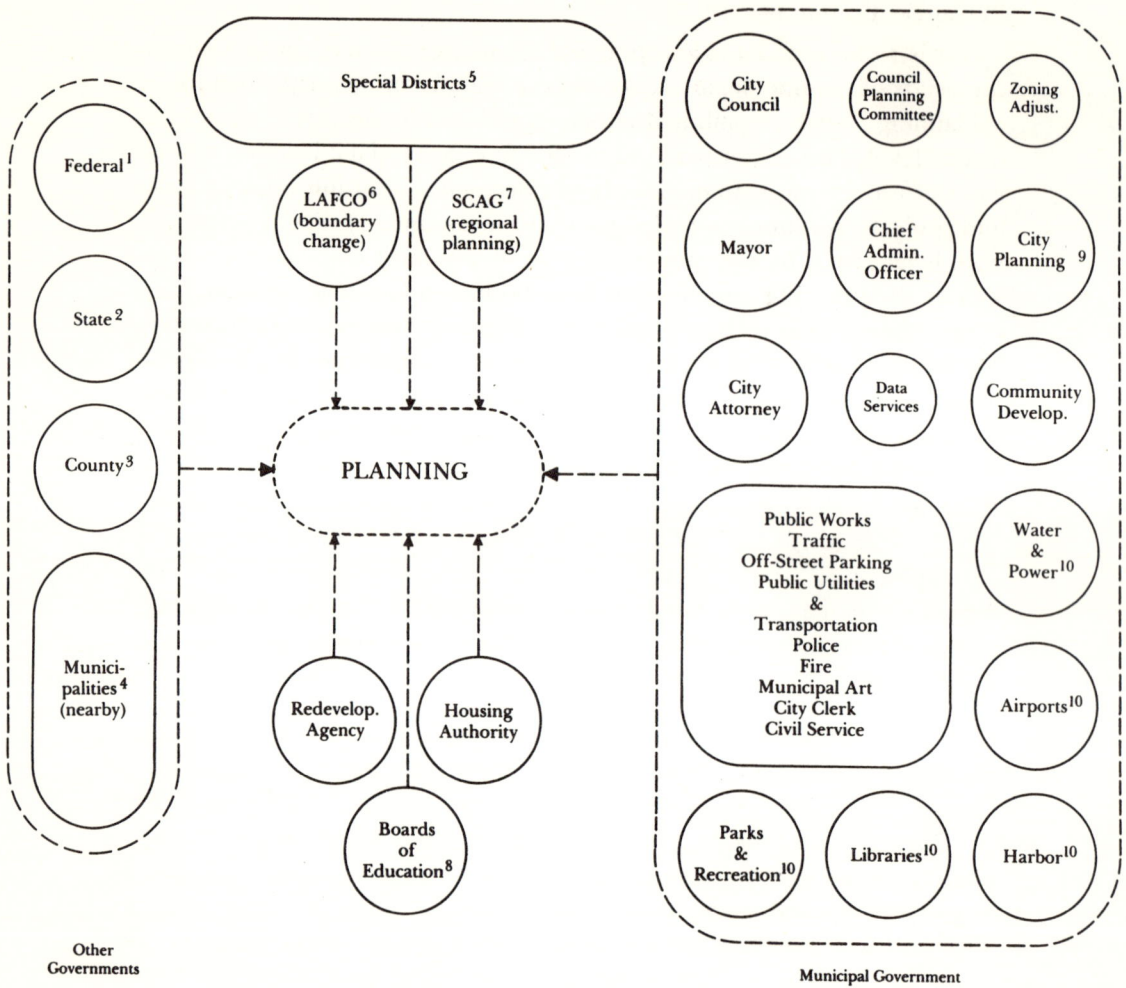

Figure 2 Participants in planning the municipality (Los Angeles, California).

The governmental units shown are some of those conducting or affecting aspects of city planning in Los Angeles, California. There are other units not shown whose effect is less direct and normally has less impact. As readily seen, traditional city planning represented by the commission and department (9) plays a relatively minor role.

Examples of ways in which certain of the units shown affect city planning are listed below for each footnote reference on the figure.

Other cities may have different organizational units, but their coverage of municipal functions and the relative importance of traditional city planning are approximately equivalent.

1. *Federal*: housing, urban redevelopment, planning process (Department of Housing and Urban Development); air, water, noise, and other pollution control (Environmental Protection Agency): federal highways (Department of Transportation); airports (Federal Aviation Administration); flood control, harbor works (Corps of Engineers); court decisions affecting the conduct of city planning (Appellate and Supreme Courts); location of physical facilities.

2. *State*: planning enabling act; state highways; preservation of agricultural land; environmental protection; coastal management; state superior, appellate, and supreme court decisions affecting the conduct of city planning; location of state physical facilities.

3. *County*: tax assessment; public assistance; health services; planning for unincorporated territory; special districts, location of county physical facilities.

4. *Municipalities* (nearby): highway and utility location and connection; land use; property tax; special districts.

5. *Special Districts*: water supply and treatment; sewerage and sewage treatment; flood control; rapid transit; air pollution; lighting; others.

6. *LAFCO*, Local Agency Formation Commission: approval of changes in local governmental boundaries and new incorporations.

7. *SCAG*, Southern California Area Governments (regional planning): recommendations to the federal government concerning its grants-in-aid and programs for various local government facilities and services.

8. *Boards of Education*: school location and related land uses; school bus transportation.

9. *City Planning*, City Planning Commission and Department: master plan; district plans; zoning; subdivision.

10. *Water & Power, Airports, Harbor, Parks & Recreation, Libraries*: self-governing departments controlling their own funds.

Figure 2 *(Continued)*

Conversely, city planning commissions regard the activities and functional plans of municipal operating departments as irrelevant to their end-state city plans. Or they believe that departmental plans should be made to conform to whatever is required to carry out their master plan. Most city planning commissions have paid little attention to municipal departmental plans. Even when occasionally city planners regard departmental plans as a desirable part of master city plans, rarely have they been able to get the municipal departments to join with them in the long-range planning process. (Note 3)

Integrating the components of any organization is never easy. The heads of separate units compete with each other on many scores: personal achievements, the record of the unit they direct, approval of plans, salaries and bonuses, titles, reputation, prestige, and perquisites. This competition is considered inevitable and constructive from a management viewpoint, an essential ingredient of corporate success.

Invariably, each unit head requests proportionately more resources for his or her unit than the parent organization can provide. This is to be expected, since naturally the managers of separate units are convinced of their own unit's capabilities and prospects, want bigger and better things for "their people," and would not have reached their position were they not personally ambitious and managerially aggressive. But some plans may conflict with those of another unit. Or there may be opportunities for coordination or cooperation that are not recognized by individual unit heads. At times, the usual activities of a unit may create a serious problem for the parent institution, unless they are planned with corporate compatibility in mind, are modified to fit, or are carried out to be supportive rather than conflictive. Such over-all problems and opportunities are not apparent to the heads of separate units because they identify with the unit which is their immediate responsibility.

It has long been an established principle of administration, management, and command that the activities and plans of the different units constituting a business, military, or other organization must be integrated in planning for the organism as a whole. "Top management" or the highest executive or commanding authority is responsible for this integration. It is accomplished for cities by *comprehensive city planning,* for large business enterprises by *corporate planning,* and for the military by *general staff planning.*

Another reason for the schism between city planning commissions and departments on the one hand, and the municipal operating departments on the other, is the original assumption that introducing outstanding private citizens into the local governmental process as city planning commissioners would bring greater integrity and loftier civic objectives to city hall. And for a brief time in some places, they probably have. But city planning commissioners are employed or engaged in private pursuits which are their main interest. With few exceptions they serve without pay, spending at most one day a week at city hall. Few have had previous education or experience in city planning. Often there is a rapid turnover of commission members, since most of them do not regard the task as a long-range opportunity or obligation—unless, as unfortunately occurs, membership provides the opportunity to enhance their own purely personal self-interests.

It is not surprising, therefore, that full-time elected and appointed municipal officials and civil servants consider city planning commissioners as uninformed missionaries, or at best as intruders or outsiders who must be tolerated. They question not only city planning commissioners' motivation and capability to perform adequately part-time, but suspect that there is an inherent conflict of interest between the private affairs of commission members and the public policies and plans they are asked to generate, and the governmental decisions they must make.

> An important element in the weakness of city planning commissions lay in the fact that they consisted of citizens who had no knowledge of planning and found little time to devote to their duties. . . . some planning agencies consider themselves watchdogs of the administration rather than advisory bodies to the mayor and council and . . . consequently, hostilities develop between the mayor and council, on the one side, and the planning commission on the other. In most instances where there has been successful planning, it came about through the development of close working relationships between the executive officer of the planning agency and the mayor, the council, the city manager, and other city departments. (Merriam, 1950)

> The use of the unpaid citizen commission, overlapping terms to eliminate "political" influences, emphasis upon published reports and "selling" specific proposals to the public, and the ill-defined status of the planning agency in the administrative structure all point to the failure to resolve the question of whether planning is a public or a private function. The efforts of public planning agencies to operate as though they were private advocates of public policy has led them, haplessly, into the political arena. There they have suffered the fate of the early Christians among the lions. (Walker, 1950)

These questions concerning the effectiveness of city planning commissions assume added importance if one agrees that "The city planning department [and commission] should be a great co-ordinating agency, intimately contacting every municipal department" (Pfiffner, 1940).

We are not considering a single functional area but the over-all coordinated action that is essential for efficient management. It is an axiom of comprehensive planning that it must be effected *within* the organism for which it is intended. Management science concluded long ago that planning for any business organization or activity must be conducted by the top executive in the organization or activity involved—if the planning is to be successful or realized at all. Every military commander plans the operations of his command, subject to strategic or tactical directives from higher authority.

Comprehensive city planning cannot be conceived and directed successfully by commissions and departments that are considered "outsiders" by the "regular" municipal departments. Nor will city plans prepared by outside consultants to city planning commissions and departments be accepted by municipal governments, for the reasons noted below. If the motivation and procedures exist within the city, it will do its own comprehensive city planning. If they do not, city plans by outside consultants will not change the unfavorable situation for planning.

Without the thorough knowledge of the organism attained only by working full-time within the municipal government, an outside expert cannot comprehend all aspects of the situation needed for sound city planning. And those within the municipality do not believe that he can acquire all the knowledge necessary for comprehensive planning without experience in the city government as a full-time participant. Nor are they likely to provide the outside part-time consultant with the most intimate operational information and entrust him with the municipality's most crucial planning activity.

These limitations apply only to the generalist type of consultant required for comprehensive city planning. Specialists supplying expert knowledge on one of the many specific and technical subjects required in most activities will make positive contributions as they always have. And more and more of them will be needed as cities become more complex and the knowledge required for their successful functioning becomes more technical and specialized. Nowadays, most technical and professional activities benefit from occasional consultation with foremost experts. But this is not likely to occur in comprehensive city planning until it is more widely established as an activity and recognized as a field of knowledge.

Whether politics in government is the "art of the possible" or the "lowest common denominator of compromise," it can hardly be ignored in city planning that professes to deal with reality and attain demonstrable results. City planning practitioners are well aware of the extent to which politics determines the nature and content of city plans. City planners are in fact staff to the elected council members or elected officials who are the municipal decision-makers, but most city planners regard politicians as powerful adversaries, if not natural enemies.

For their part, most politicians ignore unrealistic end-state city plans, because they do not deal with the crucial and usually controversial problems which are foremost in the minds of constituents and therefore the politician's primary concern. Politicians view traditional city plans as relatively meaningless, and tolerate them if they are not potentially harmful to their political careers. They will use city plans to their political advantage and do not hesitate to revise or reverse them when this is called for by developments in the real world of changing activities, issues, events—and politics. Above all, politicians avoid commitments that could haunt them at reelection time—especially any commitment to master city plans, which they consider ephemeral.

> The construction of the Beverly Center, a fact, points up the frustration of the city's planning process. . . . The mall, in effect, will become a major retail focal point on the West Side, what planners call a city subcenter. The city's general plan calls for 56 such centers. . . .
>
> However, the area where the Beverly Center is rising is not one of the communities designated as a center in the city plan.
>
> The center concept, approved by the Planning Commission in 1970 and by the City Council in 1974, forms the basis of the city's general plan. . . .
>
> "You might as well throw [the general plan] out the window if the city is going to allow big malls to go anywhere developers want them to go. . . ."
>
> "No one thought such a center would go up there. Still, I think we could have blocked it and saved the concept plan if the councilman for the area wanted to. . . ."
>
> "I preferred the project," said [the councilman of the area]. "I thought it would aid the economic vitality of the community. And besides, it was zoned for it. . . ."
>
> No one in the Planning Department suggests that the Beverly Center

should be stopped because it is inconsistent with the city's general plan. (Kaplan, 1979)

[Author's additional comment: Nor is anyone suggesting that one of the fifty-six centers designated on the plan be deleted because an unplanned center is being added.]

Political decision-makers must be made a part of city planning if it is to be meaningful. If this is not accomplished, the politicians will continue to conduct the minimum city planning possible by uncoordinated *ad hoc* decisions on individual matters as they come before them, without bene-fit of an established process in which they are directly involved from the beginning, and without the evaluative support of a city planning staff that can provide the facts, figures, analyses, and recommendations they need.

6. *Past city planning has presumed that it can avoid the primary, most pressing, and most difficult urban problems.*

Traditional city plans in the United States have not incorporated rec-ommendations directed toward resolving such primary problems of cities as poverty, unemployment, housing shortages, destructive social behav-ior, environmental pollution, and most recently the energy crisis. Deter-mining what to do about such fundamental problems is extremely difficult. It is much easier to avoid these intensely political and contro-versial problems than to confront them in city planning. And city plan-ners, when developing a master plan for a city for the first time, often copy existing master plans, none of which have considered the most criti-cal urban problems.

They have been ignored for several reasons. They are far beyond the scope and analytical competence of traditional city planning. It is not now possible to incorporate solutions for these primary urban problems in the end-state condition of the city conceptualized in traditional master plans. The knowledge for such a formulation does not exist. No one knows today what will develop in the future. No one can say what could be done specifically during the next twenty years to resolve such intrac-table problems as poverty and unemployment. They are so fundamental and persistent that small incremental progress is all that is normally pos-sible in a lifetime, or even in several lifetimes. (Note 4) Such incremental advance does not fit the concept of an idealized end-state.

Since the primary problems of cities are almost always politically controversial, specific recommendations by the city planner would associate him permanently with one of the adversative sides of the issue and impair his reputation as an objective professional person, even his usefulness as a staff planner. He would be subject to direct challenge from another side of the issue, aggressive confrontation in the inevitable power struggle involved, and possibly vigorous efforts to remove him or her from the arena of conflict.

Because city planners have ignored or been unable to contribute significantly to the gradual resolution of primary urban problems, they are not taken seriously by governmental decision-makers who are forced by events or their constituencies to face these difficulties continually and do what they can about them.

The question of the best organizational role for city planners is the subject of some debate. Most of their professional peers see them functioning most successfully as "staff" to decision-makers, providing the latter with the information and analysis they need. In this staff capacity, they can work for different decision-makers, even those with different professional convictions or different political persuasions. Some observers consider this too passive a role and believe that city planners should function in a "line" capacity, making decisions themselves as departmental general managers, city managers, or legislators, rather than attempting as "staff" employees to remain analytically objective and noncommittal concerning what should be done. Whatever their position, they should express their convictions on all matters.

City planners can indeed perform in either of these ways if they have the qualifications for the particular role. But, of course, only one of these roles can be performed at a time. Planners cannot be both line and staff at the same time, although as decision-makers they would undoubtedly want staff planners as supporting personnel. But, in any of these roles, to be effective the city planner must treat the primary municipal problems.

7. *Master city plans are conceived and issued as inflexible printed publications, revised and republished only at long intervals, regardless of changing conditions and events.*

Without exception, traditional master city plans have been printed documents, usually oversize, typeset or mimeographed, book- or spiral-bound (Figure 3). The preparation and production of these documents

I. 1918

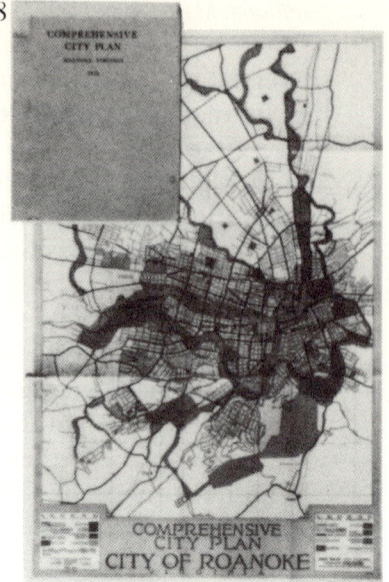

2. 1928

5. 1956

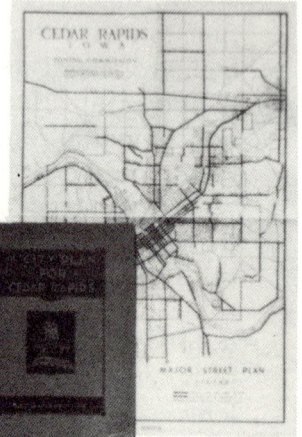

3. 1931

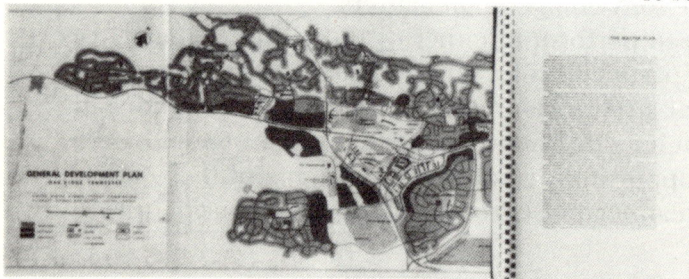

4. 1948

Figure 3 Examples of traditional city plans, 1918–1978 (Shown at the same scale and in chronological order).

6. 1959

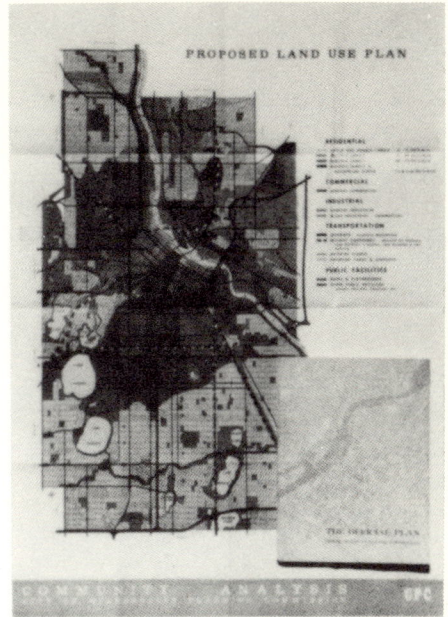

8. 1962

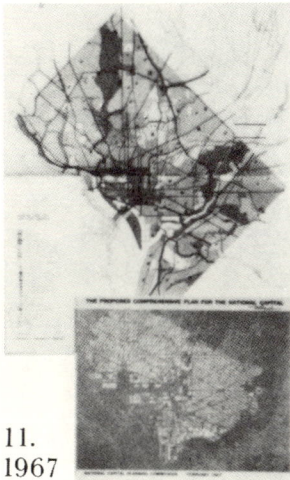

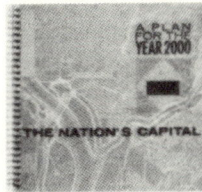

7. 1961

9. 1963

10. 1965

11.
1967

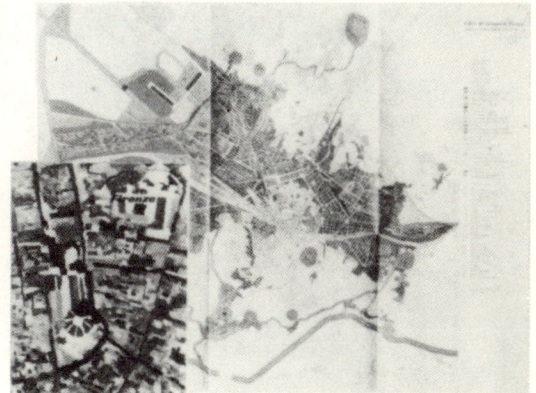

Figure 3 *(Continued)*

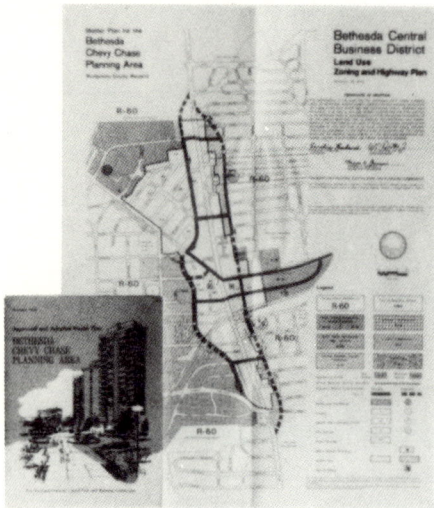
14. 1970

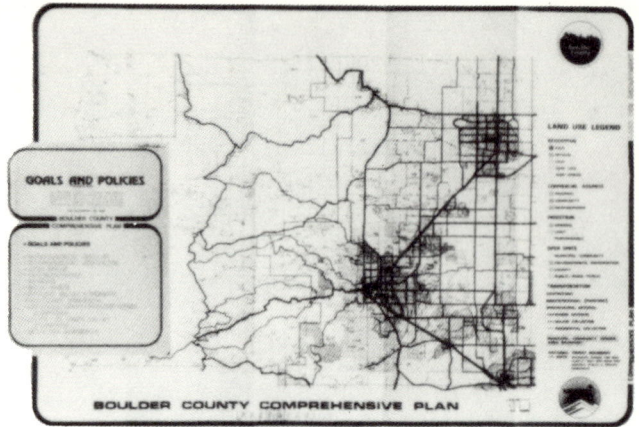
17. 1978

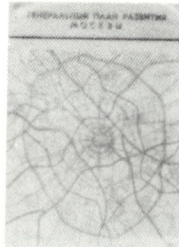
15. 1971

16. 1971

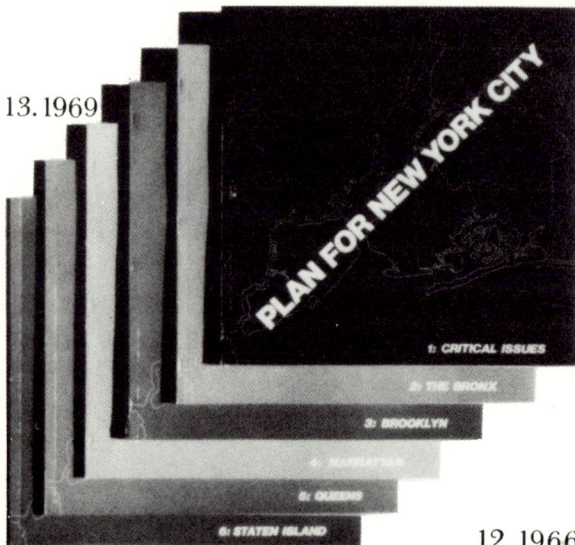
13. 1969

PLAN FOR NEW YORK CITY

1: CRITICAL ISSUES

2: THE BRONX

3: BROOKLYN

4: MANHATTAN

5: QUEENS

6: STATEN ISLAND

WASHINGTON NEW TOWN
MASTER PLAN

12. 1966

76

1. *Pro Helsingfors*, Eliel Saarinen, Helsinki, Finland (Osakeyhtiö Lilius & Hertzberg), 1918, 18 pp., foldout map-plan, map-plan insert.
2. *Comprehensive City Plan, Roanoke, Virginia*, 1928, 76 pp., foldout map-plan, map-plan inserts.
3. *A City Plan for Cedar Rapids* [Iowa], 1931, 154 pp., map-plan insert.
4. *Master Plan, Oak Ridge, Tennessee*, December 1948, 102 pp., foldout map-plans.
5. *Land Use Plan, St. Louis* [Missouri], 1956, 30 pp., foldout map-plan.
6. *Oakland* [California] *General Plan*, 1959, 7 pp., map-plan insert.
7. *A Plan for the Year 2000, The Nation's Capital* [Washington, D.C.], 1961, 114 pp.
8. *The Official Plan* [Milwaukee, Wisconsin], Fall 1962, 80 pp., map-plan insert.
9. Firenzi 1963: Problemi e Piani Urbanistici *(Urban Problems and Plans)*, Florence, Italy (Estratto dal n. 39 della Rivista Urbanistica), 1963, 46 pp., foldout map-plan.
10. *Plan Generalny Warzawy*, Warsaw, Poland (Plansze Barwne, Rysunki i Wykrisy), 1965, 179 pp.
11. *The Proposed Comprehensive Plan for the National Capital* [Washington, D.C.], February 1967, 230 pp., foldout map-plans.
12. *Washington New Town Master Plan and Report*, Washington, England (Washington Development Corporation), December 1966, 135 pp., map-plan insert.
13. *Plan for New York City, 1969*, A Proposal: 1. *Critical Issues*, 181 pp., map insert (Land-Use Policy); 2. *The Bronx*, 155 pp.; 3. *Brooklyn*, 193 pp.; 4. *Manhattan*, 171 pp.; 5. *Queens*, 155 pp.; 6. *Staten Island*, 65 pp.
14. *Approved and Adopted Master Plan, Bethesda–Chevy Chase, Planning Area*, October 1970, 40 pp., map-plan insert.
15. *Comprehensive Plan, Gatlinburg, Tennessee*, May 1971, 109 pp., foldout map-plans.
16. [*Master Plan, Moscow, Union of Soviet Socialist Republics*], 1971, 72 pp.
17. *Goals and Policies, An Element of the Boulder County* [Colorado] *Comprehensive Plan*, March 1978, 127 pp., map-plan inserts.

Figure 3 *(Continued)*

takes time: about a year to write the manuscript, prepare illustrations, and complete the other requirements of collective authorship; and another year to typeset, proofread, print, and bind the books.

This process is so expensive that a substantial percentage of the budget of a city planning department is required to print and distribute the necessary number of copies. An extreme example is the last master plan for New York City, which was issued in six lavishly produced volumes and sold for ninety-five dollars (New York City Planning Commission, 1969). Very few organizations and individuals, other than those directly concerned, could afford to purchase the entire plan at this price. And the costs of production prevented printing enough copies for widespread distribution. (Note 5) Ironically, it was almost immediately disclaimed by the very body that produced it:

> Master Plan. DEAD AT THE AGE OF 3, UNLOVED. After years of hullabaloo and hearings, the controversial Master Plan for New York City was quietly buried by the agency that proposed, pushed, and praised it, the City Planning Commission. . . . The ambitious plan, developed over a period of three years at a cost of nearly a million dollars, . . . attempted to analyze the character of the city's 62 planning districts and to suggest development of each. . . . In addition to community criticism, . . . two factors seem to be behind the reversal: New York has changed since the plan was conceived; . . . necessary federal financing, $5.5 billion a year for 10 years, is not forthcoming." (Gupte, 1973)
>
> [Author's additional comment: This ill-fated plan was produced after thirty-one years with no plan.]

A fatal flaw in this form of master plan is its inflexibility. It is outdated before it is published because of the one to two years it takes just to prepare the manuscript and print the document. And its cost precludes issuing revised versions every several years. The average time between successive printed master plans of cities in the United States is about ten years.

> The last comprehensive plan [for Dallas, Texas] was done in the early fifties, and an attempt to update it a few years ago was . . . a "disaster." (*Planning*, 1979)
>
> The master plan was outdated. . . . Planning must be a continuous process. (Zuccoti, 1973)

Besides the conceptual invalidity of end-state city plans discussed ear-lier, any sound recommendations they contain are already two years out of date by the time the plan is published. Inevitably, their relevance is further diminished as conditions change and unexpected events occur. Opponents can easily show that whatever data were used in their formu-lation are so seriously outdated that they are no longer credible. A few years after publication the plans are of so little use that most are rele-gated to the shelves of municipal and university libraries, where unfor-tunately they may be mistaken by students and other interested individuals as examples of master city plans to be emulated.

During the long interval between traditional city plans, thousands of separate decisions are made and actions taken by municipal government and private enterprise. This occurs without regard to an up-to-date city plan nor any organized body of comprehensive information and analysis that can serve as a basic reference during the protracted period while the next plan is being formulated. Interim decisions concerning city plan-ning are therefore necessarily based on fragmentary data, out-of-date in-formation, disjointed efforts to correlate different urban elements and functions, and attempts by concerned decision-makers to visualize the city as a whole. The fact that thousands of separate decisions are made in the long interval between master plans is prima facie evidence of the futility of end-state plans.

Time is of the essence in city planning. The physical city, its economics, population, social and political characteristics, and the impact of events outside its borders are constantly changing. Population mobility in some sections of larger cities in the United States has reached the point that one-half of the inhabitants of the district move away every five years, to be re-placed by new people. Urban activities have been speeded up by widespread mass communication and rapid technological advance. Increas-ingly, events far beyond city limits affect the municipality significantly. Cities are now not only growing in size and complexity, but are becoming more dynamic. City planning which cannot provide answers or ideas in time, but repeatedly postpones action until a master plan is signed, sealed, and adopted, cannot direct the development of real communities. It is an operation after the fact, a tidying up of the results of actions or events with which it has had little or nothing to do. It becomes the voice of the dis-appointed afterguard, crying in the wilderness after others have won, lost, or more usually drawn the battle. Figuratively speaking, city planning as presently conducted in the United States is not running to catch up, but is falling further and further behind at a walk. (Branch, 1970)

It should be noted in passing that the use of electronic data processing and electronic display, technically possible today, is no guarantee that city planning is up to date. The use of computers cannot compensate for misconceptions and built-in delays in the process of planning. Past city planning could have been up to date all along, had not keeping current been completely contrary to the end-state concept and therefore neither considered nor desired.

CONSEQUENCES: DIRECT AND INDIRECT

Although there have been a few exceptions to the above generalizations regarding master city planning in the United States, they correctly describe past and present practice. While they are not relevant to planning new towns during their construction, they apply when the new town becomes a self-governing municipality with its own city planning activities.

One consequence of the way planning has been conducted is that few master city plans have directed the development of cities. Most city planning staffs estimate privately that their departments are responsible for shaping not more than 5 to 10 percent of municipal growth and development. Nevertheless, the illusion persists among city planners that the end-state concept has been right and the record of ineffectiveness wrong. Why have city planners deluded themselves and misled municipal clients so consistently and for so long?

In part, this may reflect the historical thread of Utopian thinking in city planning that has persisted throughout the centuries, unrealistic objectives, or missionary zeal with respect to feasible attainments. Certainly, end-state plans have provided employment for city planning personnel for extended periods of time. A city planning department can spend ten years producing an end-state master plan, another ten years on its successor plan, and a final ten for the last plan before the time arrives for those who worked on the first plan to retire.

Of course, Utopian thinking is not to be shunned. Idealized conceptions contribute to human thought and help resolve philosophical, ethical, and social goals and choices. They encourage imaginative thinking and stimulate us to invent and aspire beyond the obvious and mundane. But Utopias and planning objectives are very different by definition. Utopian thought involves a degree of idealism, an imaginative freedom of thinking beyond the constraints of practicality or the likelihood of attainment, even ideas rejected or disliked by most people. By contrast, planning objectives are developed by projecting from the present into the future; their achievement must be possible. Realism rather than idealism is the fundamental motivation, although disciplined imagination is definitely part of background thinking. It is this requirement of realism that multiplies both the analytical and practical difficulties of city planning. Fashioning an imaginary future is not hard. It can be highly subjective and individualistic. But to determine planning objectives that are demonstrably desirable in the public or majority interest, that represent the maximum the organism involved can realistically attain, and for which a program of effectuation can be formulated—this is one of society's most difficult endeavors.

City planners share the general human tendency to forget, deny, or attempt to transcend reality. To wish urgently, to hope excessively, to imagine, to dream and daydream, to fantasy—these are necessary if humans are to cope with their unique awareness among animals of the rigors and inevitabilities of existence. Wishful imagination is, of course, an important ingredient of literature, art, music, and most fields of human knowledge and endeavor. But city planners are obligated, by the definition of the field and its basic purpose, to minimize unrealistic thinking to the extent possible in their staff role, and to make their analyses and recommendations in terms of optimum reality and objectivity.

Since most community plans throughout the 8000 years of city planning history have been drawn for rulers who had the power to carry them out, this may account for the frequent presumption by city planners that democratic societies should be able to act with royal-like centralism and fiat. But the difficulties of analyzing an organism as complex as a city are compounded in democratic societies, where the desires and legal rights of so many individuals, groups, organizations, and institutions are actively involved. It is not surprising, therefore, that some city planners are attracted, knowingly or unknowingly, to end-state master plans incorporating what the professional staff believes is desirable, making favorable assumptions concerning trends that are still unclear, basic questions that are still unresolved, and powers of effectuation that are not yet available.

Part of the end-state concept—and probably a partial reason for its existence—is the predilection among city planning personnel for complete and absolute study (witness the planning board of Pharaoh Nwab'i Ch'ow in Stephen Helburn's allegorical satire). Confronted regularly with problems requiring rapid analysis and conclusion, city planners still want to investigate each and every matter thoroughly. They would like to trace every problem back to its earliest origins, examine all its ramifications, and thereby justify to their own satisfaction whatever conclusions they reach. This quest for intellectual or analytical absolution is not characteristic of business and military planning staffs.

Several fallacies are inherent in this approach. First, complete and absolute study of any matter is theoretically impossible because of the infinite interconnections among innumerable related matters we know to exist. Second, even if total study were possible, by the time it was available the urban problem would be aggravated beyond solution, would have resolved itself in the interim without benefit of the study, or enough would have occurred during the long wait for complete study to greatly reduce the range of feasible action. Third, trying to find out everything is prohibitively costly. The time and resources available for planning are always limited. Finally, those for whom the planning was undertaken originally are disillusioned and angry when the planning process is much too slow to meet their needs.

Contributing to the professional preference for the fixed plan, despite its defects and unlikely acceptance, has been the unwillingness or inability of traditional city planners to incorporate mathematical probability in master plan analysis. It is much easier to avoid these abstractions than to deal with them. Most people prefer absolutes to uncertainties. Also, in many instances, reliable statistical data, methods of analysis, or necessary mathematical formulations are not available.

In general, it seems difficult for city planning personnel to evaluate as best they can without pretense of completeness, to deal with uncertainty, to reach a conclusion by a deadline. Often, the time requested for study seems more for the purpose of bolstering the self-confidence of the investigator than meeting the needs of the planning problem or situation. At times, it appears as if city planners are engaged in pseudoanalytical motions intended to avoid reaching a conclusion until they are confronted with a *fait accompli.*

Of course, rigorous and prolonged study is desirable in city planning, but the crucial requirement is to optimize the product of the limited time and money available. This calls for a sense of reality: recognizing when a conclusion must be reached; organizing the information available to elucidate the question at hand; selecting techniques of analysis suitable to the situation; working as comfortably with uncertainties as with fancied certainties; and being willing to act on a best guess when this is indicated.

The urge for exhaustive study can be part of the broader "avoidance" syndrome noted earlier in this section. The critical questions are somehow always deferred for further study, or postponed in favor of less consequential matters. Professional city planners are predisposed to "slip the punch" of the basic and most challenging urban problems by ignoring them, hoping they will go away, passing them on to anyone else, or avoiding them by engaging in study without end and therefore without resolution and recommendation.

Attempting to analyze urban problems completely is impossible for another reason. With the scope of city planning expanding to include more than a few physical elements, understanding their separate and interdependent dynamics becomes progressively less reliable as additional elements and aspects are added. The interrelationships among components multiply exponentially as the components increase in number. These interrelationships are even more numerous and complicated when short-term and long-term plans are considered together. It will be a long time indeed before there is reliable analysis for this far more complex concept of the city. (Figure 4) Until this knowledge is developed, the concept of end-state master plans is all the more untenable. (Branch, January 1978; Savas, 1978)

The quotation below reports the same conclusion, first, in the particular language of management science and mathematical modeling, and second, in plainer English but with less specific content. These paragraphs from *the same source* illustrate the problem of language in a field such as comprehensive planning, which draws on different disciplines. It is always important, and often difficult, to determine what a statement or formulation in the language of a particular discipline really means, and what it contributes to the body of knowledge concerning comprehensive planning.

When applied to public-sector planning, traditional least-cost optimization models and their offspring, contemporary multiobjective models, have often been developed under the optimistic philosophy of obtaining "the answer." Frequently, such models are not very useful because there are a multitude of local options, which result from wavy indifference functions, and because important planning elements are not captured in the

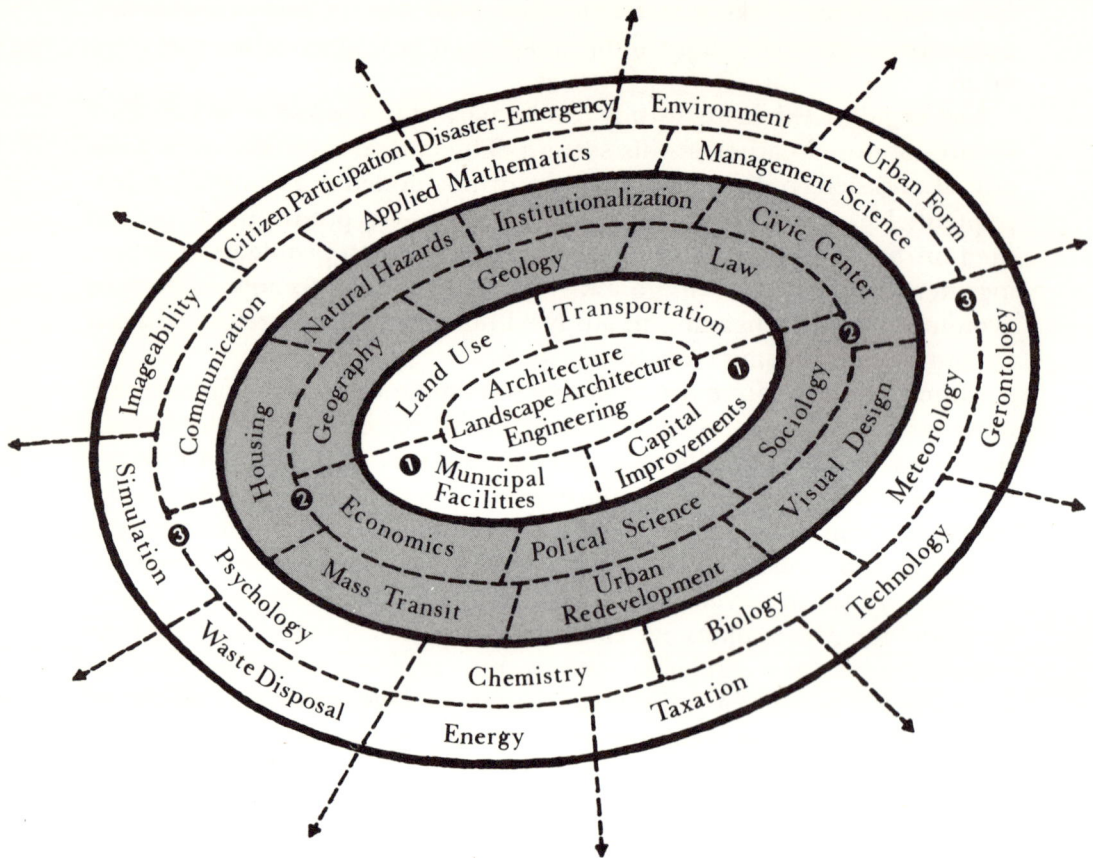

Figure 4 The expanding universe of urban planning analysis. ① Early development, 1900–1940. ② Intermediate period, 1940–1965. ③ Present period, 1965–.

formulations. Omitted elements, in fact, may imply that an optimal planning solution lies within the inferior region of a multiobjective analysis instead of along the noninferior frontier. The role of optimization method should be re-thought in full recognition of these limitations and of the relevant planning process. . . .

There are likely to be difficulties, of course, in achieving complete representation of a planning problem using a mathematical formulation. Many issues cannot be satisfactorily quantified, and others may not be well un-

derstood. Other issues may be discovered well after the planning process
has begun. (Brill, 1979)

Useful theory has been developed for certain urban elements that are
limited in scope and are covered by a single or several closely related disciplines or fields of knowledge. Traffic flow theory, for example, has pro-
gressed with the contributions of applied mathematics and several
engineering specializations. Location theories, based on studies of market requirements, have been developed by private enterprise for certain
land uses. In the United States, the separation of one or several similar
land uses into separately zoned areas reflects an implicit theory that this
promotes stability of property values. Neighborhood theory as first developed by Clarence Perry has been applied to almost all new towns, and
is advocated by some as the way new peripheral and redeveloped central
areas of cities should be spatially organized. There are theories with respect to urban taxation, population growth, electric power distribution,
social stratification, smog generation, and many other urban elements.

For comprehensive city planning to be scientifically sound, existing
theories concerning single elements must be analytically combined, integrated with other elements when theories are developed for them, and
ultimately fused into a reliable analytical formulation that explains the
city as a whole greater than the sum of its parts.

> No intellectual discipline can establish itself and progress very far with-
> out a firm theoretical base. Without theory . . . : sound generalizations can-
> not be made; experience must be re-learned repeatedly; entirely new
> situations must be approached without general guidelines; and the body of
> knowledge comprising the discipline has no continuous structure of coher-
> ent logic and conclusion. Only bits of such a theoretical structure for city
> planning now exist. . . .
>
> It looks like three groups of theories—systems analysis, scientific man-
> agement, and urban dynamics—will inspire and eventually coalesce to form
> comprehensive city planning theory. The first of these groups involves
> general systems theory, systems engineering, operations research, and ap-
> plied mathematics. The second includes business [and public] administra-
> tion, management science . . . decision, communication, and organization
> theories, applied psychology. Theories concerning the planning process,
> advocacy planning, and the decentralization of planning belong to this cat-
> egory. The last group consists of the theories . . . which relate to the form

and dynamics of urban communities in physical space. Of course, it will be a long time before this synthesis takes place. . . . And nowhere should sound theory more likely evolve than from observation of real cities and close contact with their planning, far and away the best "experimental laboratory" available. (Branch, 1970)

After sound urban theory has been formulated, reliable analytical knowledge can be developed concerning the functioning of the most significant urban elements, first separately, and then together with their many interconnections. This will take time and require the most intensive effort by the very best minds representing at least the several different fields of knowledge suggested in the quotation immediately above. A team approach is required. The intellectual task is beyond any individual mind, although undoubtedly individual minds will make major contributions.

As noted in Part One, architects, engineers, and landscape architects were the chief students and practitioners of city planning in the United States throughout the first half of this century. The first two of these professions have been pre-eminent in community planning since its beginning. Landscape architects exerted considerable influence on urban design during the Renaissance. Architects and engineers are now outnumbered on urban planning staffs by professionals from various fields directly involved in planning cities, such as economics; sociology; geography; environmental, health, computer, and management sciences; applied mathematics; and law. Most fields and professions are now concerned in one way or another with some aspect of comprehensive city planning, municipal management, urban research, and urban studies as they are broadly defined today.

The historical dominance of architects and engineers in city planning has favored the end-state type of city plan. Professionals in both of these fields draw complete plans of what they are designing, in sufficient detail not only for clients to see what they are considering, but to provide precise specifications, allow cost estimates, and permit bidding and construction. In times past, only one ruler or a very few powerful persons had to be satisfied in order for the urban projects to proceed. And since they were physical installations that did not involve socioeconomic concerns beyond the project site, the scope of consideration and the plans of architects and engineers were limited to the three-dimensional entity that was to be the final product. It was understandable, therefore, for them to approach plans for cities in the same way that they approached individual projects. But the project plan approach was invalid for entire communities from the start—all the more so as cities became larger, more complex, and less amenable to authoritarian decision-making. The engineer abandoned inappropriate applications of the end-state concept in city planning much sooner than the architect, probably because engineering projects are usually more utilitarian in nature and more subject to cost considerations.

Today, city planning is being done for the most part by the large and growing number of professionals whose graduate education has been in this field. They come from many different academic backgrounds. But they have transferred from their previous field of concentration to city planning, recognizing that there are not enough hours in the day to keep up in two different fields of knowledge simultaneously and perform in two areas of professional practice at the same time. It is this group of city planners who should be the catalysts for the development of comprehensive urban planning theory and analysis. They must use knowledge and ideas from allied fields—economics, political science, law, systems engineering, and many others—but the product of their work must be more than an amalgamation of theories developed by and for closely related fields. It must be specifically for cities and their planning, but it must incorporate principles and procedures that will be applicable to planning more generally.

Several fields of knowledge and applications of planning in practice will contribute to the development of a body of theory and a set of principles that can be applied generally in comprehensive planning. Urban and regional planners will deepen their analytical understanding of the cities and regional areas with which they are associated. Management scientists, corporate planners, and operations researchers will gradually extend their capacity to plan, with quantitative and mathematical precision, certain single functions and subsystems of several closely related activities. They would like to include many more diverse components in their analysis and still maintain its mathematical rigor. Similarly, applied mathematicians seek to extend the range of their calculative capabilities. Public administrators would like to integrate long-range planning with their customary shorter-range operational capabilities. And social scientists and psychologists are striving to learn more about individual, collective, and organizational behavior. Military planners are finding it necessary to expand the scope of their analytic consideration to cope with cold war, nuclear standoff, "crazy states," and hostilities conducted via the mass media of communication. From those different fields will gradually accumulate the capability of planning more comprehensively and more reliably.

The most devastating delusion or confusion of all would be to underestimate the magnitude of the city planning endeavor. What is being attempted is most ambitious in its implications and difficulties. Planning runs counter to a number of rigidities and natural tendencies in Man. Recognizing and facing reality is fundamental to planning. Yet, Man's capacity to face unvarnished facts and avoid purely wishful thinking is discouragingly low. It is not innately easy for people to forego present needs and desires for future benefits which they may not even enjoy because they accrue to the next generation. Coordination does not come easily to people. Psychologically, Man tends to be a "lonely island"; biological and social bases for cooperation evolve slowly and often painfully. . . . Man prefers certainties to uncertainties, a bird in the hand to several in the plan. In general, he resists frequent and extensive change. Planning sets higher standards and calls for continuous improvement, requires greater effort. To the average individual, it seems easier to plan as little as possible, rather than as much as suggested. Finally, planning presupposes and requires a reasonable triumph of rationality over instinct and emotions, of order over disorder, of constructive hope over discouragement or fatalism.

Hope based on Man as he really is has better cause to spring eternal than if it is founded on delusion or fanciful thinking. City Planning is a constant struggle against human traits, societal features, and other realities which require it to be a gradual, relentless process. Incremental advance, not rapid or radical change, is the normal expectancy. Undertaking too much prevents significant achievement on the smaller, cumulative scale of reality; it can also discredit planning in the eyes of decision-makers, beneficiaries, and other beholders. Overzealousness or resentment because matters progress slowly or not as fast as the staff would like, antagonizes friends and potential allies, wears and tears the frustrated city planner apart, and ultimately results in everyone's disadvantage. City planning in the United States is many things, but analytically and operationally it is most analogous to a never-ending game of chess played against tough opponents, requiring the strategy, plans, and tactics of a grand master to win. (Branch, 1970)

The process and mechanism described in the next section of this book are required if city planning is to be a fact rather than a pretense. Although it will be some time before reliable comprehensive city planning

analysis is achieved, the mechanism proposed for continuous city planning provides the means of stimulating and advancing analytical knowledge. To the extent possible, it represents the real city and its dynamics.
It reveals what is known and not known about the interrelationships
among different components of the city. The relatively simple analytical
methods proposed permit limited conclusions heavily dependent on human judgment, and they disclose areas of ignorance and provide a base
from which more advanced methods of analysis can be developed step
by step. Therefore, the simulation of a city and its planning represented
by the mechanism proposed in the next section of this book can be used
to advance our knowledge of planning as well as for its application in
practice.

NOTES

1. Besides being appropriate to the subject at hand, this reproduction of most
    of the text of possibly the last available copy of Stephen Helburn's essay as
    it was originally typewritten is a fitting memorial to a brilliant young "plan-
    ner" who had the courage to challenge the existing master planning process
    as well as to surmount the handicaps of a paraplegic confined to a wheel
    chair. He died in 1940, having lived less than thirty years.

    Rereading this commentary every few years is refreshing and therapeutic.
    It promotes appropriate modesty and reminds urban and regional planners
    of several of the profession's most serious intellectual and occupational haz-
    ards. It reminds us how often the same delusions and fundamental mistakes
    can occur over and over again.

2. A relatively recent development in Atlanta, Georgia, is an exception:

    > In 1974, as a result of a new charter and departmental reorgan-
    > ization, Atlanta institutionalized a process by which the Compre-
    > hensive Development Plan becomes the major policy statement of
    > how the City will manage its resources. As far as [Mr. Eplan] can
    > tell, it probably represents the most far-reaching attempt in local
    > government, not only to establish a full planning/budgeting sys-
    > tem at that level, but also to use The Plan as the Central Statement
    > of Governance.... Under the reorganization of the Executive
    > Branch, a new bureau was set up, called the Bureau of Budget Poli-
    > cy and Evaluation, and was placed with the Bureau of Planning
    > into the Department of Budget and Planning. (Eplan, Leon S.,

"Administering the Comprehensive Plan," Address to the American Institute of Planners, Kansas City, Missouri, 8 October 1977, typescript, pp. 5 and 8)

3. The single exception to this generalization known to the author is the Planning and Management Support System of the Cincinnati City Planning Commission, which

> ...gathers information on current planning activities of all agencies, whether inside city government or not, and classifies the planning work of these agencies by type; that is, by subjects and by phases. It portrays who is doing what and how far they have progressed. It classifies implementation action projects in the same manner. This would enable management decisions to be made with the full knowledge of planning policies and objectives, if there were any, and would tell what planning should be undertaken, if there were not any. [Kleymeyer, John E. and Hartsock, Paul, *Cincinnati's Planning Guidance System,* Planning Advisory Service Report No. 295, Chicago (American Society of Planning Officials), October 1973, p. 1]

4. A notable exception is the rise in the average family income of the comparatively small populations of many of the Oil Producing Export Countries (OPEC), brought about by the billions of dollars they have acquired through the sale of oil.
5. The 1969 *Plan for New York City* was also an extreme example of the mistakes that have been made in "packaging" printed master plans. Each of the six volumes is too high to fit upright on ordinary library shelves, and is so wide in its other dimension that the volume's center of gravity does not allow it to be placed flat on ordinary library shelves without falling off. When stacked on a table one on top of the other, the plasticized covers are so slick that a slight jar causes the volume on top to slide off the others.

REFERENCES

Barron, James T., "Advising the President," *Princeton Alumni Weekly,* 24 November 1975, p. 11.

Batey, P. W. J. and Breheny, M. J., "Methods in Strategic Planning," *Town Planning Review,* Vol. 49, No. 3, July 1978, p. 263.

Branch, Melville C., "Delusions and Diffusions of City Planning in the United States," *Management Science,* Vol. 16, No. 12, August 1970, pp. B-715–B-716, B-727–B-728, B-729–B-730.

Branch, Melville C., "Critical Unresolved Problems in Urban Planning Analysis," *Journal of the American Institute of Planners,* Vol. 44, No. 1, January 1978, pp. 47–59.

Branch, Melville C., *Comparative Urban Design, Rare Engravings, 1830–1843,* New York (Arno), 1978, p. 68.

Branch, Melville C. and Robinson, Ira, "Goals and Objectives in Civil Comprehensive Planning," *Town Planning Review,* Vol. 38, No. 4, January 1968, pp. 261–274.

Brill, E. Downey, Jr., "The Use of Optimization Models in Public-Sector Planning," *Management Science,* Vol. 25, No. 5, May 1979, pp. 413, 415.

Bromage, Arthur W., *Introduction to Municipal Government and Administration,* New York (Appleton-Century-Crofts), 1957, pp. 401, 411.

Cantril, Hadley, *Gauging Public Opinion,* Princeton, N.J. (Princeton University Press), 1944, pp. 228, 230.

Cowan, Edward, "Getting Rid of Obstacles to Business Efficiency," *The New York Times,* 24 December 1972, Section 3, p. F3.

Drucker, Peter F., "The Deadly Sins in Public Administration," *Public Administration Review,* Vol. 40, No. 2, March/April 1980, p. 103.

Gupte, Preney, *The New York Times,* 10 June 1973, Section 4, p. E4.

Kaplan, Sam, "A Commentary on Planning: Frustrating the City's Planners," *Los Angeles Times,* 7 October 1979, Part IX, pp. 1, 6.

Karachi Development Authority, with the assistance of the United Nations, *The Karachi Development Plan 1974–1985,* Final Report, Pilot Project 3, Karachi, Pakistan (Master Plan Department), August 1974, p. vii.

Lamson, Newton W., "Plots Thicken for Corporate Planners," *The New York Times,* 13 April 1975, Section 3, pp. F1, F11.

Lieder, Constance, "Lieder on AIP's Future: Focus on Substance, Not Organizational Structure," *AIP News,* Vol. 12, No. 8, November 1977, p. 1.

Los Angeles Times, 18 March 1975, Part II, p. 6.

Merriam, Charles E., in Robert A. Walker, *The Planning Function in Urban Government,* 2nd ed., Chicago (University of Chicago), 1950, pp. ix, x.

Meyerson, Martin, "Building the Middle-Range Bridge for Comprehensive Planning," *Journal of the American Institute of Planners,* Vol. XXII, No. 2, Spring 1956, p. 62.

New York City Planning Commission, *Plan for New York City, 1969:* 1. *Critical Issues,* 181 pp. with map insert; 2. *The Bronx,* 155 pp.; 3. *Brooklyn,* 193 pp.; 4. *Manhattan,* 171 pp.; 5. *Queens,* 155 pp.; 6. *Staten Island,* 65 pp.

The New York Times, "The Need to Plan . . . for Economic Policy," 23 February 1975, Section 4, p. E12; "The Case for Government Planning," 16 March 1975, Section 3, p. F14.

The New York Times, 5 December 1976, p. 38. See also: Adrian, Charles R., and Griffith, Ernest S., *History of American Government: The Formation of Traditions,* New York (Praeger), 1976, 233 pp.

Otten, Alan L., "Politics and People," *The Wall Street Journal,* 19 December 1974, p. 12.

Pfiffner, John M., *Municipal Administration,* New York (Ronald), 1940, p. 377.

Planning, "New Dallas Planning Chief," Vol. 45, No. 9, September 1979, p. 24B.

Savas, E. S., "New Directions in Urban Analysis," *Interfaces,* Vol. 6, No. 1, November 1978, pp. 1–9.

Sheldon, Eleanor Bernett and Parker, Robert, "Social Indicators," *Science,* 16 May 1975, pp. 693–698.

Stein, Herbert, (Chairman, President's Council of Economic Advisors) in Soma S. Golden, "Nixon Aide Hints Need for Agency to Plan Economy," *The New York Times,* 30 December 1973, Section 1, pp. 1, 28.

U.S. National Resources Committee, *Our Cities, Their Role in the National Economy,* Report of the Urbanism Committee, Washington, D.C. (United States Government Printing Office), June 1937, p. 63.

Vidal, David, "Colombia Is a Nation in a State of Urban Crisis," *The New York Times,* 9 October 1977, Section 4, p. E3.

Walker, Robert A., *The Planning Function in Urban Government,* 2nd ed., Chicago (University of Chicago Press), 1950, p. 364.

Walsh, John, "Looking Out for Science Policy," *Science,* Vol. 209, No. 4458, 15 August 1980, p. 783.

Wolman, Abel, "The Metabolism of Cities," *Scientific American,* Vol. 213, No. 3, September 1965, pp. 178–188, 190.

Zuccotti, John E. (Chairman, New York City Planning Commission), "City's [sic] Planning Panel to Start Workshops for Neighborhoods," *The New York Times,* 10 June 1973, p. L 44.

Part Three

CONTINUOUS CITY PLANNING

A different process of city planning and a different kind of master city plan must gradually replace both the end-state concept that portrays the city as planners believe it should be years hence, and the after-the-fact plan that simply indicates what capital improvements are planned by municipal governmental units, with little or no modification from the viewpoint of over-all comprehensive city planning.

BASIC CONCEPT AND GENERAL IMPLICATIONS

In the new form of city planning, the plans of different municipal departments are correlated so that they are mutually supportive, rather than actually or potentially inconsistent or even in conflict. Thus, a new automotive maintenance facility for one city department might be located where it could serve another department in off-peak periods; two separate maintenance facilities might use a single repair unit; or two municipal hospitals could share a costly diagnostic unit that neither could afford separately. The gathering of closely comparable statistical information by several municipal departments can often be combined with only insignificant modification to serve their respective purposes at much less cost.

This kind of coordination is never easy to achieve. The different units of organizations almost always claim that their requirements are unique and that any modification for any purpose will seriously impair their operations. Despite this expected reaction, the single most essential requirement of comprehensive planning is integration of the different elements of the organism involved.

In continuous city planning—unlike in traditional city planning—certain elements of the city are projected far into the future, others into the mid-range, some into the near future, and a few are not projected at all. The primary highway network of a city can be expected to function for a long time, since the capital investment is so large, the acquisition of rights of way so protracted, and construction times so long that significant change in the system is effected only very gradually over a period of half a century or more. By contrast, the life of some buildings is limited by the type of construction, maintenance or rehabilitation costs, changes in the operations of the activities they were built to house, or other characteristics or conditions. Some elements of the city, such as the cost of borrowing money or the actions of some governmental units, can be reliably projected short-term at best. And at times a few elements of the city—such as public attitudes, political outcomes, or economic forecasts—cannot be reliably projected at all. They must be left indefinite or projected within a range of upper and lower limits. In continuous city planning, no pretense is made that the representation or simulation of the city that serves as its analytical base is intellectually or analytically complete. As noted previously, such completeness is beyond human capability at present for organisms as complicated as cities.

Planners tend to use the words *planning* and *plans* interchangeably. In discussing continuous planning, it is important to differentiate between the two terms. Plann*ing* is the process of continuously formulating what the municipality is able to and intends to carry out with respect to its future—as up to date as needed for this purpose. Plans, on the other hand, indicate the actions to be taken during a prescribed period of time to achieve stated objectives. Planning is the continuously moving picture, composed of a succession of master plans analogous to the individual picture frames of the motion picture.

> The traditional concept and practice of "town planning" or "master planning" . . . has been associated with a concept of a "plan" that is far too static. Typically a "master plan" has been prepared and then updated every five to ten years. . . . Such master plans often are out of date by the time they are published. They do not provide a means by which the many agencies that must contribute to sound metropolitan growth can interact throughout the planning and development process. Master plans cannot be a substitute for having as a permanent part of the machinery of government a planning process through which data on the condition of the Metropolitan Area are kept current and through which policies, long-range plans and specific action programmes are evolved continually in response to current needs. (Karachi Development Authority, 1974)

Continuous master city plans are not the traditional printed document depicting the city planner's concept of a desirable end state for the city twenty or more years in the future. As noted later, they may be reproduced as documents, but in a much faster and less expensive form than traditional plans. Because they incorporate the budgets, operating plans, and longer-range objectives and goals of the municipal departments, they are sufficiently representative of the actual condition and intentions of the municipality to permit a level of effective planning otherwise unattainable. The process of continuous city planning is shown in Figure 5.

As indicated schematically, master city plans are adopted at the begin-

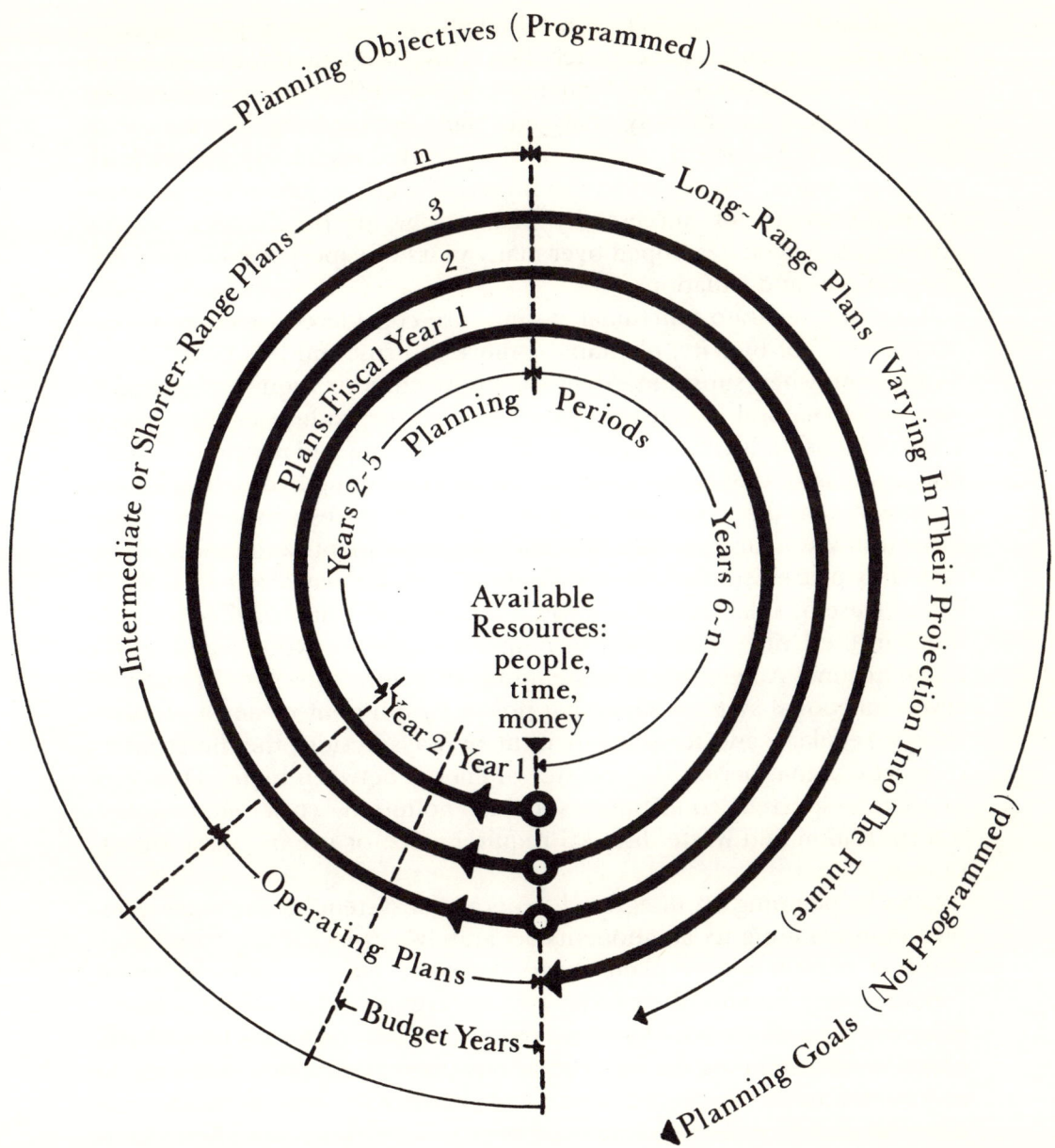

Figure 5 Schematic representation of the continuous planning process.

ning of each year, together with a budget and operating plan. Specific plans and programs for their effectuation are formulated for those activities, projects, functions, or elements that are sufficiently circumscribed to be precisely and reliably analyzed. Many engineering systems are in this category. Municipal utilities can be planned separately with considerable precision. For example, the financial, legal, engineering, and other requirements for successfully planning water or electrical supply systems have been developed over many years of experience in many different places and situations.

But when separate functional systems are considered together as one "subsystem" of the city, planning is more difficult and less exact. As an illustration, when substandard air quality conditions require the temporary use of natural gas instead of oil or coal to produce energy, a new interrelationship is created between these polluting and nonpolluting energy systems, and between them and any nonpolluting hydroelectric generating system that could supply power. This requires considering these three utility systems together. But nuclear power plants and power plants fueled by processed garbage and flammable waste may also be involved. Greater use of solar energy is also underway, and some smaller communities in the United States are turning once again to wood as a fuel for home heating. An energy subsystem may therefore consist of as many as seven functional systems supplying power by different means, but interrelated regularly and temporarily in many ways besides the direct interconnections that permit the transfer of energy between them. They vary in their respective contributions to air pollution, cost, vulnerability, transportation and waste disposal requirements, or use of public rights-of-way.

Clearly, planning an integrated "energy subsystem" is far more complex than planning its components separately—especially now that accidents at nuclear power plants have increased the possibility of major contamination because their safety systems are not as fail-safe as claimed. Solar energy collectors on rooftops require preserving access to sunlight, which in turn requires zoning regulations preventing a new structure or an addition to an existing structure from casting its shadow on an existing solar energy collector. The solar energy subsystem could be extended further to include the measures now being taken to conserve energy by reducing the large heat losses in buildings as presently designed and constructed, or by reducing lighting standards which are higher than necessary to prevent eye injury.

It can be seen from these examples that planning a number of interrelated functional systems as an integrated subsystem produces analytically sounder and operationally better planning for the entire organism. This is the basic logic of comprehensive planning: gradually to incorporate more and more elements within an analytical construct that makes possible more successful direction of the organism. Since we cannot yet successfully analyze and plan comparatively simple utility subsystems, it will be a long time before we can integrate the overwhelming number of elements involved in truly comprehensive planning. Compounding the difficulty, most of these are variable, many are indeterminate.

The end-state concept of the master plan is therefore all the more impossible, since it not only assumes integrative knowledge far beyond present capabilities, but the additional capability to accurately forecast the development of each significant element separately and to project the future state of all of them in concert. Until we have such abilities, a flexible and continuous system of planning is required.

There is wide variation in how much is known about the different elements of a city, the extent to which they can be quantified and analyzed separately and in combination, and their likely development over time. With the necessary data, municipal population growth can be analyzed and projected with considerable accuracy. On the other hand, no known technique, including the Delphi technique of consulting experts, enables us to forecast when new technologies might be used in a city. Desalinization of seawater to provide potable water is used on a small scale at various locations around the world, but it is not yet economically feasible for municipal use in the United States. Linear induction transportation systems have been built and tested, but these magnetically suspended and propelled vehicles have not yet proven practical for cities. Even the monorail, which has been operating since 1901 on a short haul in Wuppertal, West Germany, has not fulfilled the widespread and repeated recommendation by planners that it be used as the backbone of urban mass transportation systems.

Municipal systems are most difficult to plan when they are composed of different urban subsystems. For example, the primary highway network in a city is related to the secondary street system, railroads, water transportation, airways, pedestrian ways, and bicycle paths. Also involved are pipelines, which are also part of the municipal energy subsystem, because they carry materials that would otherwise have to be transported in vehicles. The maintenance and future development of the urban transportation subsystem is dependent on municipal taxes, bonds for financing capital improvements, federal, state, and county subventions and grants—all part of the municipal financial subsystem. With each such additional interconnection with another subsystem, over-all analysis and planning become progressively more difficult.

Since all components of organisms are interrelated directly or indirectly in some way, the sequence of interconnection can be extended until logically all elements of the city must be taken into account when considering any one of them. Because we cannot pretend to do this for a very long time, complete or end-state planning is impossible and continuous city planning must be applied.

"Policy planning," which has been advanced in recent years as a new academic concentration by political scientists, planners, and others, presupposes that the planning process is continuous. As intentions signifying general directions of development, policies do not indicate how a goal will be achieved. This is revealed and decided as circumstances develop and opportunities occur. As Henry Kissinger has commented, "Policy emerges when concept encounters opportunity." Policies are different from "planning objectives" which are precisely stated with specific programs for their attainment (Branch, Robinson, 1968). The indefiniteness of how policies will be implemented is in sharp contrast with the specificity of the projected condition, completed project, or other programmed achievement of plans. Both policies and plans are inherent parts of continuous planning.

To a much greater extent than traditional planning in the past, continuous city planning incorporates current data, analyses, and information concerning a wide variety of conditions and relevant events. Long-range plans represent the outcome of a succession of actions and anticipations rooted in the past, beginning or continuing in the present, and directed toward the future. It is analytically invalid as well as indefensible in practice to formulate longer-range plans without working out how they are derived from present conditions and developed through the intermediate future. The absence of this necessary interconnection between long-range plans and current conditions is the main reason traditional end-state master city plans have been so unsuccessful.

Traditional town planning and the preparation of traditional "schemes" fail to recognize the project cycle through which initial development ideas are translated into feasible plans, funded, implemented, operated and monitored. It is a cycle which requires not only the formulation of long-range objectives and plans but also specific project feasibility analysis and design, the mobilization of public and private resources, physical construction and programme implementation, follow-up to check and evaluate actual development and, on the basis of this, an updating and improvement of programmes as planning and development continue. (Karachi Development Authority, 1974)

Certainly, city planning cannot assume the operating functions of municipal departments such as protection of persons and property, public works, building regulation, transportation, or social welfare. Day-to-day management and longer-range planning for such municipal activities are each a full-time task. Centralizing the planning of too many different components—or even supervising the plans of these units too closely—is self-defeating. Rarely is there enough knowledge to successfully plan large and complex organisms centrally, with minimum decentralization of functional management and planning. Attempting to do so requires such a large accumulation of central staff that the organization becomes top-heavy, subordinate managers have little motivation and authority, and the organization as a whole is less productive. As a general rule, the smaller the comprehensive planning staff, the better.

City planning should be the central mechanism for synthesizing—not formulating—the operations, budgets, and functional plans of the different departments, with relation to the total city system and its projected future. In this respect, the master city plan and the corporate business plan serve the same purpose of integrating the plans of different groups, divisions, or departments of the organization. Their separate budgets, operating plans, and longer-range functional plans are incorporated—often after modification and occasionally after revision—in the master city plan or corporate business plan.

> Our whole system of management [Texas Instruments, Inc.] is geared to planning on a continual basis. . . . Our quarterly rolling plan covers one to three years out into the future. (Pearson, 1977)

Effective city planning encompasses the temporal spectrum of consideration extending from the past, through the present, toward the future: obligations springing from past actions, immediate needs, and long-range commitments; tactics and strategy; certainties and uncertainties. Some elements, such as major freeways and primary water supply lines, are projected fifty or more years into the future. Some, such as land use in certain areas, may not be planned more than a few years ahead, awaiting developments. Others, such as changes in restrictions on outdoor advertising, in the policies of private lending institutions investing in urban land and real property, or in the forms of government subsidy and incentive, may at times be difficult or impossible to forecast.

Because they seek to formulate an end-state for the city, traditional plans have brought about a serious misconception concerning "objectives" in city planning. Many people assume that long-range objectives must be determined at the outset or planning cannot commence. And it is true that planning, by definition, must be directed to some purpose, explicit or implicit, short-term or long-term as the case may be. But long-range objectives that are obtainable and not illusory are determined only after examination of the natural and physical resources available to meet existing commitments and support future developments. Resources committed in the past or allocated today to support current programs are not available to achieve longer-range objectives. Objectives are an extension into the future of activities begun in the past and actions taken today. Setting objectives is a "circular" process with neither a fixed beginning nor an assured end, as indicated conceptually in Figure 5. They are prospects for the future shaped by the realities of the past and present.

Continuous city planning incorporates information, analysis, and projection into the future for each principal urban element, separately and as an integrated pattern of actions, plans, and objectives which will benefit the city as a whole. The master city plan is maintained and displayed in such form that it can be revised regularly, and changed completely and quickly if need be. It is always sufficiently up to date to serve as the basic analytical representation of the municipality, and the official reference for discussing and deciding most city planning matters. It is ahead of the game rather than running to catch up. To function in these ways, the master city plan cannot be so restricted by bureaucratic or legislative formalities that the necessary combination of established objectives and flexibility is impossible.

Master city plans must be formulated in a far more current, dynamic, and flexible manner than the traditional booklets and brochures which have been revised only every ten years on the average. The first step in attaining this objective is a mechanism of analysis and exposition that maintains a constantly up-to-date formulation of information that simulates the state of the city. It incorporates material depicting the planning effort: policies, goals, objectives, functional and comprehensive plans, and programs of accomplishment. This material changes continuously with changing circumstances, events, developments, and decisions. Some time in the future this simulation for city planning purposes may be handled entirely on output-display devices connected with electronic computers and videotape storage systems, but this will be a long time coming as explained at some length later in this book.

The mechanism for conducting continuous city planning must be accepted and used by the municipal officials responsible for directing the affairs of the city: the city council, executive officers of the city, and municipal department heads. It must, therefore, reflect their operating needs. Otherwise, they will be unable or unwilling to use it in connection with their respective activities and for comprehensive planning of the city as a whole. Nor can the mechanism be so complex or require such special capabilities for its use that those for whom it is intended cannot or will not use it. Ordinarily, executive decision-makers will not base their decisions on a method of analysis and evaluation whose underlying principles and critical features they do not personally understand. Since effective interaction between municipal operating officials and city planning departments has not often been achieved in the past, obtaining it in the future will require deliberate effort to this end.

Recently, judicial decisions and state legislation in the United States are beginning to require that master city plans coincide with zoning maps. As noted previously in this book, ever since the first comprehensive zoning ordinance in New York City in 1916, zoning maps have usually served as the primary reference for city planning decisions. The formulation of master city plans took so long and they were so out of date when published that they could not be used as guides. They either portrayed an end-state too unrealistic to be used, or little more than a few physical features from the operating plans of municipal departments. Both the trend toward mandatory adoption of master city plans and the impossibility of formulating and maintaining up-to-date traditional end-state city plans are exemplified in the following situations. Clearly, the situation reported to exist in Florida indicates that continuous city planning is required if comprehensive city plans and land-use regulations are to be legally consistent and mandatory comprehensive planning is to be enforced.

> The comprehensive plan plays an increasingly important role in land-use litigation. The plan, once an advisory document, has assumed the status of law in some states.
>
> As of July, 1979, 14 states have adopted mandatory planning legislation. In 12 of them, land-use regulations or public works projects must be consistent with local plans.

In two states, planning is optional, but consistency is required if there is a local comprehensive plan.

In still other states, the courts measure the reasonableness of local land-use regulations in terms of their conformity to the plan.

Even in states that mandate planning and consistency, plans are rarely challenged and struck down. However, there are exceptions. . . .

In states that have statutory or judicially imposed consistency requirements, the courts will usually define consistency to mean compatibility with or comformity to plan policies, objectives, or goals. Consistency generally does not mean that the zoning map must be identical to the plan map. . . .

Usually, considerable deference is given to a local planning agency's finding of consistency. (Netter, 1980)

Every municipality and the unincorporated area of every county [in Florida] must adopt a comprehensive plan by July 1 of this year [1979]. . . . If they don't, the counties are required to plan for them; and if the counties don't plan, the state must. Communities that fail to comply will be billed for the planning that is done for them; up to 50 percent of their funds from the state could be withheld for payment. And, once plans are adopted, they are subject to review every five years. . . . The adopted local comprehensive plan has legal status. All development regulations—zoning ordinances, subdivision regulations, building codes—must conform to the comprehensive plan. All building permits, rezonings, subdivision approvals, special exceptions, and variances must conform. . . . Neither the local government nor the state can build a facility unless it accords with the local comprehensive plan. . . .

Nearly four years after passage of the [Local Government Comprehensive Planning Act] . . . fewer than 10 percent of Florida's communities adopted comprehensive plans. . . . The plans themselves range from the fold-out map submitted by the city of Miami to the 550-page plan produced by the city of Baldwin, population 3,000. (Lewis, 1979)

State legislation has been proposed that would require local governments to enact and "freeze" city plans for several years; only during short intervals between the fixed periods could changes be made (California Legislature, 1980). So ingrained is the tradition of end-state city plans that the primary professional organization of urban and regional planners in the state supported this legislation that would arbitrarily force local governments to use the kind of master plan that has been discredited by the experience of the past half century. Master plans fixed for two years and traditional city plans projecting an end-state twenty or more years in the future, differ only in the time periods during which they are frozen in an unrealistic rigidity.

Because artificially frozen plans violate the realities of natural events and human affairs, they preclude continuous planning by preventing the flexible functioning of government considered necessary and desirable by most societies. The capacity to change is required by the many unpredictable events and unexpected developments that occur randomly but repeatedly in real life. It is difficult to imagine a local government in the United States that would willingly forgo its right to modify its prior actions and plans, shift direction, or even engage in capricious change. The right to change if and when the legislature decides it is desirable is a fundamental prerogative of each level of democratic government, as well as a realistic requirement for the optimal conduct of human affairs.

Not only does continuous planning call for changes in the practice of city planning, but in urban planning research as well. In recent years, this has been conducted almost exclusively at universities. It has tended more and more toward purely abstract or artificially oversimplified studies that are divorced from the realities of cities as they exist and city planning as it functions in fact. The gap is widening between academic research and research that is meaningful for municipal planning in practice. City planning theory and background urban research that do not reflect reality belong more appropriately to a field of academic concentration other than "urban and regional planning." True city planning theory and urban research that are relevant to municipal planning in practice, however abstract their formulation, take into account the full range of significant factors intrinsic to cities and their planning. The great increase in the complexity of study and application which this broadening in scope brings about cannot be avoided.

As a consequence of this divorcement of research and practice, little of the theoretical study and academic research undertaken in the field of urban and regional planning today is concerned with city planning per se, that is, the process of formulating and implementing city plans in the actual world of people, time, economics, politics, special interests, bureaucracy, and the many other forces that constitute cities. Nor are methods of analysis being developed in academia that are understandable, acceptable, and usable by city planning decision-makers, and that improve the quality of their decisions.

One area of extensive research nowadays is mathematical modeling. Various intellectual and academic disciplines seek to quantify interactive dynamics that exist among different urban land uses, among the components of urban transportation systems, among the elements of the municipal economy, or among the diverse parts of some other urban system. Some of this research will contribute to mathematical methods of reliably analyzing the quantitative interactions among different elements and forces, thereby adding gradually to accumulated knowledge concerning the functioning of cities as a whole. But this type of background research is not now directed toward the *process* of planning, the research area of greatest need and least attention that involves organizational arrangements, analytical methods that are readily understood, procedures for effective decision-making, means of implementation, and other operational elements of conducting city planning in real life.

The different purposes and uses of background research as opposed to operational research are illustrated by land-use planning for the California desert areas owned by the federal government and managed by its Bureau of Land Management (BLM). Large parts of the desert were being overrun by off-road recreational vehicles (ORVs), causing long-lasting or irreparable damage to the natural environment. Unique archaeological sites were also being carelessly or wantonly destroyed.

First, the soil type and vegetative cover of the many thousand square miles of desert land involved were mapped from data obtained by remote sensing from an orbiting satellite more than 500 miles above the earth. The interpretative validity of the data was checked by comparison with "ground truth." Soil and vegetative analyses were combined to provide a "biomass" index, which measured the number of "animal units" of commercial grazing that could be supported by different desert environments without serious damage to their natural condition. To acquire the same background information by ground survey would have been prohibitively expensive for the BLM, and large sections of the desert would have been irreversibly damaged during the much longer time required to develop the data in this way.

These remotely sensed data were correlated with other information concerning topography, land use, archaeological sites and on- and off-road vehicular circulation, which was obtained from high altitude defense mapping and lower level aerial photography. These data were available because of past research, extending over many years, in physics, mathematics, optics, chemistry, metallurgy, electronics, and other fields underlying the photographic and electromagnetic scanning devices employed and the aircraft and spacecraft that carry them aloft. Because of this *background research,* the BLM could determine more precisely and reliably which areas were most subject to environmental damage.

Although it was probably known from experience what kind of land-use controls were needed, scientific data were lacking that would convince decision-makers to impose the necessary regulations. It was also essential to determine exactly what rules to impose, how to secure conformance, how to obtain the cooperation of state and local government agencies, how to monitor compliance and enforce controls, and what additional knowledge was needed to carry out a land-use plan for the federally owned California desert.

On one side, ORV users and manufacturers and others benefiting from their unrestricted use constitute a special interest group with considerable political power. On the other side, environmentalists, hikers, and campers using existing roads are disturbed by the progressive environmental damage caused by ORVs, and archaeologists are concerned about the destruction of unique historical sites. In between, political decision-makers involved at each level of government seek to avoid any proposed plan that does not favor their self-interests. Thus, at present, how to formulate planning that will be effective calls for more thought than how to obtain additional data permitting more exact spatial delineation of environmental vulnerability. The capability of formulating feasible plans evolves from *operational research* into the processes of planning in the real world of limited resources and conflicting interests. This research would focus on such operational concerns as the best evidence supporting proposed actions to alleviate existing problems that is convincing to those involved, an appropriate form of plan that includes the necessary elements and provisions, the resolution of conflicting interests, or political, financial, legal, and managerial feasibility. (Hill, 1980)

It should be noted that background research and operational research for planning do not differ in the same way as "basic research" and "applied research," as these terms are commonly employed in the scientific community. In one way or another, background research for planning reflects a wide variety of basic research from science and other areas of knowledge. Operational research for planning reflects basic research that relates to organizational arrangements, administrative procedures and decision processes, individual and collective human behavior, and other areas relating to how planning is carried out. Because planning is a field of action as well as a field of study, applied research is relevant to both background and operational research in planning. Similarly, "theory" is involved in both background and operational research for planning: in the development of basic substantive knowledge in the first instance, and in determining the most successful planning process in the second.

ANALYTICAL CORE

An example from corporate planning illustrates the kind of analytical core lacking in present city planning. Historically, businesses have quantified their activities, made many of their decisions, and evaluated their performance on the basis of three analyses: operating statement, profit and loss statement, and balance sheet. It has long been known that these statements cover only the primary elements of the business, but they are essential simulations for the successful operation of simpler businesses. Additional information can be incorporated in these core analyses, and the accuracy of component elements and their interrelationships can be progressively improved.

The corporate core of information and analysis has expanded at an increasing rate in recent years as accounting inadequacies in the three simplified statements have been identified, applied mathematics have specified more interrelationships, electronic computers have permitted faster and more accurate quantitative analysis, and more information relating to the public sector has been included. As corporations continue to grow in size and diversity, the analytical core they must maintain for operating and planning purposes becomes ever more complex and crucial for successful management and decision-making.

While many multinational corporations now employ as many as several hundred thousand people working in many different enterprises in numerous countries, they are not as difficult to manage and plan as a city. Corporate ownership is of course limited, management control more absolute, motivations and interests simpler, and factors to be considered far fewer. Nevertheless, the principle of a core of information and analysis applies equally to public affairs, municipal management, and city planning. Without it, public management is inefficient if not chaotic, and city planning is ineffective if not a delusion. Every planning activity needs a core of information and analysis to provide facts and a basis for calculation. Its contents may be extensive, formally specified, and kept up to date. Or in its simplest form it may exist only in the mind of the decision-maker. It is no less essential for sound planning because it is incomplete and uncertain. Were complete knowledge required before any action could be taken, nothing would be accomplished. We are always acting on partial knowledge.

The analytical core for city planning should incorporate only those elements and their interactions that can be formulated with the requisite reliability. This means that the core will expand gradually, since each additional element requires determination of more interactions. It is preferable to work with an analytical core composed of fewer elements that can be reliably formulated than with one containing more elements, many of whose interactions cannot be accurately quantified and correlated. In this way, confidence is maintained in the analytical core itself, whether or not the information and analysis it contains is modified in the minds of decision-makers by their consideration of additional elements and interactions that the core does not contain. If so many elements were included that the calculative accuracy of the analytical core were weak or questionable, decision-makers would reject it for this reason alone. They are much less likely to reject it if it is limited and makes no pretense of completeness.

Primary Elements

Continuous analysis begins with deliberate modesty. First, the most important functional elements of the municipality are identified. Surprisingly, the voluminous literature of city planning contains no conclusions or consensus concerning the elements most necessary for comprehensive planning. Multitudinous city planning studies are made, producing all together a vast quantity of data, but no priorities can be deduced from this output concerning what should be analyzed first.

Figure 6 illustrates a set of primary elements that most people will agree are basic to realistic city planning. Surely, the *population* of a municipality and *housing* are paramount elements. For the city to exist and function, *land uses* are established that closely relate to the *circulation* of people and materials in and about the city. These elements are part of all traditional city plans. *Economic* and *financial* factors are obviously important if the city is to survive and remain socioeconomically healthy, but they have been ignored by traditional city planning in the United States, except when recommendations are occasionally made concerning the capital works program. Rather than planning in terms of available funds and their allocation, city planners have ignored financial constraints, or have assumed that someone would somehow procure the funds they claim are needed. In sharp contrast, continuous city planning is conducted in terms of the *source and application of funds.*

Of course, a city cannot exist in a reasonably healthy state without potable water, energy, drainage, sewerage, and solid waste disposal, provided by municipal *utilities* or in some more primitive way. While they are not mandatory and vary widely among municipalities, *facilities* and *services* for the protection of persons and property, provision of books, outdoor recreation, and various other governmental activities are accepted measures of municipal attainment in modern industrial societies. *Communications* serve urban business and commerce, constitute an important means of interpersonal contact, and in the case of radio and television affect social stability. *Public educational* facilities are no less important because they are outside the scope of city planning today. Education requires a large share of available municipal funds; its purposes are socially significant; its facilities are important transportation foci. *Health, safety,* and *environment* are not only important urban elements but also our most feasible "social indicators." They reflect the social and environmental condition of the city, the latter ignored in traditional city planning until 1970, when the federal Environmental Protection Act ushered in a new era of environmental concern and impact reports.

The *regulatory* elements of continuous city planning analysis concern its effectuation. Planning is realizable only to the extent that it is supported by society. The reluctance to do this in the United States is seen clearly in the unused directive powers provided by existing land-use controls, which now include more than thirty kinds of zoning, subdivision control, and environmental impact review; control over the location and arrangement of transportation systems, public utilities, and facilities; programming capital improvements; tax policy; and governmental subventions and grants.

Finally, since the *official city map* is the legal reference for exact cartographic location, it is perforce part of continuous city planning.

While primary elements different from those shown in Figure 6 might be selected for analysis and effectuation by different individuals or groups making this decision, and the most important elements vary among communities, a priority must be established. Everything cannot be handled at once, much less analyzed successfully. In every form of planning, only a limited number of elements can be analyzed, although one might like to include many more. And they may shift with time, events, different values, changes of objectives, emerging goals, or other developments. The major difficulty in many communities may prove to be getting the necessary information in the first place.

Information

Information must be available to represent the state of each element analyzed. This may be available from local, state, and federal governmental units, from private enterprises, or it may be gathered by the city planning agency itself. It must be available at an affordable cost. It must be reliable enough to serve the purposes intended. Its continued availability should be reasonably certain, and information should be sufficiently comparable over time to reveal trends. Quantification of the information should facilitate comparison, correlation, and projection of components.

If the data for a particular urban element do not meet most of these requirements, their use in comprehensive planning analysis should be postponed. Careful and controlled use of data for the basic urban analysis is important. City planning has been ineffective or wasteful in its use of information in the past, often indiscriminately collecting masses of data with little regard to their relative importance and the extent to which they can be correlated with other data. City planning staffs often ask for more and more information, not because it is specifically needed, but in order to prolong the process, to avoid tackling difficult but critical problems, to postpone decision-making, or in the vain attempt to collect the infinite quantity of information that would theoretically be needed for a valid end-state plan. In general, "We already have the capability to collect more information than we can fully process and analyze" (Tight, 1979).

As shown in Figure 6 in the supplementary notes and righthand columns, the basic data for urban analysis will differ: in how up-to-date and accurate they should be, whether they should apply to the entire municipality or only part of it, and how far they should extend into the past to support conclusions concerning trends. A common mistake is to alter the composition of data, not enough to improve them significantly but enough to prevent their continued use to determine trends. There is ample evidence that local governments are careless, if not sometimes deceptive, in their collection and analysis of data. Nor are state and federal governments necessarily more reliable because of their larger size and higher level. It is important to avoid the general tendency to ascribe truth to data simply because they are expressed in numbers, or because they come from "higher authority."

[Thirty] percent of [43 key American cities] could not adequately account for public money spent on land, buildings and equipment and . . . only 60 percent of the cities had their statements audited by an independent accountant. . . .

"The pervasiveness of the municipal data problem . . ." was shown by

CORE INFORMATION[a]		RECYCLE[b]	CONCEPTUALIZATION, DISPLAY, ANALYSIS, CORRELATION		
No.	**INFORMATIONAL CATEGORIES**		**PANELS**		**CORRELATION BETWEEN CATEGORIES (PANELS)**
			VERTICAL PHOTO	**TRANSPARENT OVERLAY & OTHER**	
	ANALYTICAL A. Population B. Housing C. Circulation D. Economic E. Source and Application of Funds F. Utilities/Waste Disposal G. Facilities/Services H. Communications I. Education J. Health/Safety/Environment REGULATORY K. Land Use Planning L. Density/Intensity M. Specific Plans OFFICIAL CITY MAP	EVERY: x YRS. (xY); YR. (Y); MO. (M); WK. (W)	Controlled or uncontrolled photo mosaic, or orthophoto assembly of vertical photographs: for general visualization and correlation with information on transparent overlay and other panels. They cover the urban area to be considered at three different scales.	Data shown by areal location on transparent panels (Tr). Different information shown on different panels is correlated by superposing panels displaying data at the same areal scale. A photographic (Ph) or other panel can be placed as a base reference behind transparent overlay panels at the same scale. Opaque boards (Op) can be correlated side by side with each other or with transparent overlay panels. Menuboards (Me) are used for numerical information.	Illustrative correlations between each category involved and other categories identified by number: accomplished by superposing up to 5 transparent panels, with a photo panel or other opaque panel underneath as desired, or by side by side comparison. Correlation between panels at different scales are shown in parenthesis ( ). These comparisons are made by visual inspection or the data can be programmed and correlated by computer, printed out, and displayed graphically. The correlations shown below are indicative only.
			AREA COVERED	**TIME PERIOD**	
			ENTIRE CITY (1"=4800') / SECTION OF CITY (1"=1600') / SMALL AREA (1"=400')	PAST / PRESENT / FUTURE (PLANS): YEAR 5 / YEAR 10 / YEAR 15	

Number of Vertical Photo Boards: 90[1]   1   7   82

ANALYTICAL:

A. Population (Totals by Sex and Color; Areal Spot Transparencies; Menuboards)

No.	Category	Recycle	Entire City	Section of City	Small Area	Past	Present	Year 5	Year 10	Year 15	Correlation	K
1	Total	2Y	Tr	(Me)			$(Tr)^2Me^3$	Me	(Tr)Me	Me	9,11,13,15,17,22,23,26,(29),(32)	K:ES
2	Under 6 Years	2Y	Tr	(Me)			(Tr)Me	Me	(Tr)Me	Me	(40),(42),(45)	
3	6–11 Years	2Y	Tr	(Me)			(Tr)Me	Me	(Tr)Me	Me	(35),(40)	
4	12–17 Years	2Y	Tr	(Me)			(Tr)Me	Me	(Tr)Me	Me	(35),(41)	
5	18–25 Years	2Y	Tr	(Me)			(Tr)Me	Me	(Tr)Me	Me	22,(35)(41)	
6	26–40	2Y	Tr	(Me)			(Tr)Me	Me	(Tr)Me	Me	22,(35),(41)	
7	41–65	2Y	Tr	(Me)			(Tr)Me	Me	(Tr)Me	Me	22,(35),(41),(43)	
8	66 & Over	2Y	Tr	(Me)			(Tr)Me	Me	(Tr)Me	Me	11,13,17,21,22,(35),(41),(43),(44)	

Number of Panels/Boards: 5   4   (1) $(4)^51$ (1)   (4)(1)   (1)

B. Housing (Number of Dwelling Units; Areal Location Transparencies; Menuboards)

No.	Category	Recycle	Entire City	Section of City	Small Area	Past	Present	Year 5	Year 10	Year 15	Correlation	K
9	Total[6]	Y	Tr(Me)		Tr	(Tr)	(Tr)Me	(Tr)Me		(Tr)	16,17,18,(29),(30),(31),(32)	
10	Single-Family, Duplex, Row	Y	Tr(Me)		Tr	(Tr)	(Tr)Me	(Tr)Me		(Tr)	17,21	
11	Substandard[7]	Y	Tr(Me)		Tr	(Tr)	(Tr)Me	(Tr)Me		(Tr)	17,21,22	
12	Apartments	Y	Tr(Me)		Tr	(Tr)	(Tr)Me	(Tr)Me		(Tr)	17,21	
13	Substandard[7]	Y	Tr(Me)		Tr	(Tr)	(Tr)Me	(Tr)Me		(Tr)	17,21,22,23	K:S
14	Other	Y	Tr(Me)		Tr	(Tr)	(Tr)Me	(Tr)Me		(Tr)	17,21	
15	Substandard[7]	Y	Tr(Me)		Tr	(Tr)	(Tr)Me	(Tr)Me		(Tr)	17,21,22	

Number of Panels/Boards: 86   3   82   (82)   (82)1   (82)(1)   (82)

[a]These illustrative analytical materials are conceived for cities of considerable size in countries with highly developed informational systems and services. Not only may the categories of most useful analytical information vary between countries and cities because of functional characteristics and circumstances, but accurate data may not exist for desirable categories of information. There is, nonetheless, a core of information concerning people, their dwelling places, their movement, and basic municipal services, which is of primary importance for the functioning of all cities and for which enough data are available or procurable to support constructive city planning. [b]Exceptional conditions may shorten or prolong normal recycle times. [1]Vertical Photo Boards (Panels) are not repeated under the various categories below, where they would be used repeatedly behind the Transparent Panels indicated. [2]Designations in parentheses indicate an additional element of the information shown in another column for the same category of information on a Transparency (Tr), Menuboard (Me), or Opaque Panel (Op). [3]Menuboards with numerical information. [4]K = Key Economic (E) and/or Social (S) Indicators. [5]Numbers in parentheses indicate that this information is incorporated on panels/boards previously listed and counted.

Figure 6 Illustrative analytical core. Continuous city planning process constituting the general, developmental, or comprehensive master plan.

112

RECYCLE	AREA COVERED			TIME PERIOD					CORRELATION BETWEEN CATEGORIES
	CITY	SECT.	AREA	PAST	PRES.	YR. 5	YR. 10	YR. 15	

C. Circulation (Areal Location Transparencies; Menuboard)

#	Name	CITY	SECT.	AREA	PAST	PRES.	YR. 5	YR. 10	YR. 15	Correlation
16	Autos (Personal & Commercial)	2Y	Tr			(Tr)Me		(Tr)Me		13,17,22,(45),(48),(49),(52)
17	Buses & Routes (Public & Private)	2Y	Tr			Me		Me		7,8,12,13,15,16,(21),(22),(23)
18	Trains & RR Lines (Pass. & Freight)[8]	2Y	Tr			Me		Me		21,26,(45),(49)
19	Aircraft & Fields (Comm. & Private)[9]	2Y	Tr			Me		Me		1,17,(45),(49)
20	Other (Specify)	2Y	Tr			Me		Me		-----

Number of Panels/Boards: 2   1   (1)1   (1)(1)

D. Economic (Areal Location Transparencies; Menuboards)

#	Name	CITY	SECT.	AREA	PAST	PRES.	YR. 5	YR. 10	YR. 15	Correlation	
21	Family Income (by Sex & Color)[10]	Y	Tr(Me)	Tr(Me)		(Tr)Me		(Tr)Me		5,6,7,8,11,13,15,17,22,23,(42),(44)	
22	Unemployment[11]	3M	Tr(Me)	Tr(Me)		(Tr)Me		(Tr)Me		1,13,15,17,21,23,(44)	K:ES
23	Poverty[12]	3M	Tr(Me)	Tr(Me)		(Tr)Me		(Tr)Me		1,11,13,15,17,21,22,(42),(44)	
24	Retail Sales[13]	Y	Tr(Me)	Tr(Me)		(Tr)Me		(Tr)Me		1,10,12,14,16,17,(38),(49),(52)	
25	Commercial Volume[14]	Y	Tr(Me)	Tr(Me)		(Tr)Me		(Tr)Me		1,10,12,14,16,17,(38),(49),(52)	
26	Industrial Production[15]	Y	Tr(Me)	Tr(Me)		(Tr)Me		(Tr)Me		1,17,18,22,(49)	

Number of Panels/Boards: 11   3(1)   7(1)   (3)1   (3)(1)

E. Source & Application of Funds (Menuboard)

#	Name	CITY	SECT.	AREA	PAST	PRES.	YR. 5	YR. 10	YR. 15	Correlation	
27	Sources[16]	Y	(Me)			Me	Me	Me		(10),(12),(21),(24),(25),(26)	K:E
28	Applications[17]	Y	(Me)			Me	Me	Me		(17),(29),(32),(33),(34),(35),(40),(41)	

Number of Panels/Boards: 8   (1)   1   (1)   (1)

F. Utilities/Waste Disposal (Areal Location Transparencies; Menuboard)

#	Name	CITY	SECT.	AREA	PAST	PRES.	YR. 5	YR. 10	YR. 15	Correlation
29	Water[18]	Y	Tr(Me)			(Tr)Me	(Tr)Me	(Tr)Me		(1),(10),(12),21,24,25,26
30	Electricity[19]	Y	Tr(Me)			(Tr)Me	(Tr)Me	(Tr)Me		(1),(10),(12),21,24,25,26
31	Natural Gas[20]	Y	Tr(Me)			(Tr)Me	(Tr)Me	(Tr)Me		(1),(10),(12),21,24,25,26
32	Sewage/Storm Drainage[21]	Y	Tr(Me)			(Tr)Me	(Tr)Me	(Tr)Me		(1),(10),(12),21,24,25,26
33	Solid Waste[22]	Y	Tr(Me)			(Tr)Me	(Tr)Me	(Tr)Me		(1),(10),(12),21,24,25,26

Number of Panels/Boards: 8   (7)(1)   (7)1   (7)(1)   (7)(1)

G. Facilities/Services (Areal Location Transparencies; Menuboard)

#	Name	CITY	SECT.	AREA	PAST	PRES.	YR. 5	YR. 10	YR. 15	Correlation
34	Police & Fire Stations	Y	Tr(Me)			(Tr)Me	(Tr)Me			(1),(10),(12),21,22,23,41,44,(52)
35	Libraries & Recreation Centers	Y	Tr(Me)			(Tr)Me	(Tr)Me			(1),(10),(12),(17),21,41
36	Others	Y	Tr(Me)			(Tr)Me	(Tr)Me			-----

Number of Panels: 8   7(1)   (7)1   (7)(1)

---

[6]Does not normally include hotel/motel rooms. [7]Without toilet and hot running water in the dwelling unit. [8]Average number of passenger and freight cars arriving per day. [9]Average number of aircraft arriving per day. [10]Gross income per family. [11]Persons receiving unemployment relief from any source. [12]Families receiving less than the minimum income required for subsistence. [13]Annual dollar sales. [14]Annual dollar income from commercial activities/services other than retail trade. [15]Annual dollar sales. [16]Municipal Income: property taxes, licenses, fees, fines, etc.; State: sales/gas tax rebates, grants, revenue sharing, etc.; Federal: revenue sharing, grants, projects/activities, etc. [17]General Administration, Operations, Capital Works, Education, Other. [18]Use: gallons per average and peak days; main lines. [19]Kilowatt per average and peak hours; transmission, trunk lines. [20]Cubic feet per average and peak days; primary supply lines. [21]Gallons per average and peak days; main lines. [22]Cubic yards or weight per average and peak days; disposal/recycle sites.

Figure 6 (*Continued*)

RECYCLE	AREA COVERED			TIME PERIOD					CORRELATION BETWEEN CATEGORIES
	CITY	SECT.	AREA	PAST	PRES.	YR. 5	YR. 10	YR. 15	

H. Communications (Areal Location Transparencies; Menuboard)

#		RECYCLE	CITY	SECT.	AREA	PAST	PRES.	YR. 5	YR. 10	YR. 15	CORRELATION
37	Telephones & Cable TV[23]		Y	Tr(Me)			(Tr)Me	(Tr)Me			(1),21,24,25,26,(48),(49),(52)
38	Newspaper Distribution[24]		Y	Tr(Me)			(Tr)Me	(Tr)Me			(1),(10),(12),21,24,25

Number of Panels/Boards: 1   (7)(1) [SECT.]   (7)(1) [PRES.]   (7)(1) [YR. 5]

I. Education (Areal Location Transparencies; Menuboard)

#		RECYCLE	CITY	SECT.	AREA	PAST	PRES.	YR. 5	YR. 10	YR. 15	CORRELATION
39	Total Attendance; Education Completed[25]		Y	Tr(Me)			(Tr)Me		(Tr)Me		(1),(17);,22,23,25
40	Nurseries, Elementary & Grammar School[26]		Y	Tr(Me)			(Tr)Me		(Tr)Me		(1),(2),(3),35
41	High School, University, Adult Education[27]		Y	Tr(Me)			(Tr)Me		(Tr)Me		(1),(4),(6),(7),(8),21,35

Number of Panels/Boards: 8   7(1) [SECT.]   (7)1 [PRES.]   (7)(1) [YR. 10]

J. Health/Safety/Environment (Areal Transparencies; Menuboard)

#		RECYCLE	CITY	SECT.	AREA	PAST	PRES.	YR. 5	YR. 10	YR. 15	CORRELATION	
42	Infant Mortality Adult Morbidity		Y	Tr(me)			(Tr)Me		(Tr)Me		(1),(2),(11),(13),(14),21,22,23,43	K:S
43	Hospital Beds, Physicians		Y	Tr(me)			(Tr)Me		(Tr)Me		(1),22,42	
44	Crime		Y	Tr(me)			(Tr)Me		(Tr)Me		(1),(3),(4),(5),(6),(7),(11),(12),34	K:S
45	Pollution, Cleanliness[28]		Y	Tr(me)			(Tr)Me		(Tr)Me		(1),32,33,(49),(52)	

Number of Panels/Boards: 8   14(1) [SECT.]   (14)1 [PRES.]   (14)(1) [YR. 10]

REGULATORY:
K. Transportation (Areal Transparencies; Menuboard)

#		RECYCLE	CITY	SECT.	AREA	PAST	PRES.	YR. 5	YR. 10	YR. 15	CORRELATION
46	Sts., Highways, RRs, Air Fac's			Tr(Me)			Me				(1),(10),(12),47,(48–53)
47	Parking Places, Easements			Tr(Me)			Me				(1),(12),(16),(18),(19),(48–53)

Number of Panels/Boards: 8   7(1) [SECT.]   1 [PRES.]

L. Land Use/Zoning (Areal Transparencies; Menuboard)

#		RECYCLE	CITY	SECT.	AREA	PAST	PRES.	YR. 5	YR. 10	YR. 15	CORRELATION
48	Residential[29]		W	(Me)		Tr	Me				(1),(10),(12),(46),(21),49–53
49	Commercial/Industry		W	(Me)		Tr	Me				(1),(18),(19),(45),48,50–53
50	Government/Other[30]		W	(Me)		Tr	Me				(1),(46),(47),48,49,51–53
51	Open Space/Hazard[31]		W	(Me)		Tr	Me				(1),(46),(47),48–50,52,53
52	Density/Intensity[32]		W	(Me)		Tr	Me				(1),(21),(44),(45),(46),(47),48–51,53
53	Mixed/Specific Plans[33]		W	(Me)		Tr	Me				(1),(14),(46),(47),48–52

Number of Panels/Boards: 1   (1) [SECT.]   (82)[34] [PAST]   1 [PRES.]

TOTAL Number of Panels/Boards: 70 Photo Boards and 142 Transparent Panels covering 465 sq. mi. ground area. 12 Menuboards

OFFICIAL CITY MAP[35]: (Maintained separately in municipal departments)

---

[23]Number and location of telephones and cable TV. [24]Areas of regular distribution. [25]By sex and color. [26]Location of facilities. [27]Location of facilities, attendance statistics. [28]Air pollution: ozone concentration per million parts of air; noise: L_{eq}; radiation: Roentgen readings — all on random sampling days and times. Cleanliness: trash/liter detected by visual on-site inspection of randomly selected areas, or of enlarged aerial stereophotographs. [29]Single family, apartments, and other dwelling units including mobile homes, apartment hotels, boats, other. [30]Federal, state, regional, county, municipal. [31]Open space includes: parks, other recreational areas, school athletic fields, reservoirs, agricultural land, cemeteries, vacant land and flood plains, other; but not streets, nor front and side yards required by the building code. Hazard areas are those specially zoned against flood damage, explosion, radiation, earthquake, tidal waves, other. [32]Areas with restrictions on population density, imposed in regular zoning requiring minimum lot size and front and side yards, limiting the bulk and/or the height of buildings, or by special overlay zoning. [33]Vertical zoning, planned unit development, specific plans, or other exceptional arrangements of different zones closely combined. [34]Uses same transparent panels listed for B. Housing above. [35]Base maps with the cartographic accuracy necessary for exact geographical location, engineering specification, and legal description of public rights of way, governmentally imposed boundaries, and public and private property lines.

Figure 6 *(Continued)*

114

the fact that half of [the studies of the 66 American cities] had to be excluded because too much information was missing—not only on pension fund liabilities, but on breakdowns by sources for taxes, on the uses of short-term debt or the market value of taxable property and the condition of long-term assets. (Miller, 1979)

A study of the annual financial reports of 100 cities across the nation has found "substantial inadequacies" in the reports.... Most of the reports that were examined failed to "provide the complete or clear statement of a city's [financial] health needed by investors, taxpayers and even government officials...."

More than one third of the reports were published more than six months after the fiscal year ended—too late, in the opinion of the study, for taking optimum corrective action or for serving as a basis for the next year's fiscal decisions. (Stuart, 1979)

After a 12-week study of Cleveland's management, a task force of business executives came away "appalled" at the city's lack of systems to gather information needed to make sound decisions.... The city currently is only using 40% of the capacity of its data center.... Members of the task force spent an estimated 35,000 hours on the study and would have cost the city more than $1 million if the [eighty-nine] executives had been hired instead of loaned from businesses. (*The Wall Street Journal*, 1980)

Probably the most important requirement for capital management is information on where the underground capital networks are located, what the condition of the various capital elements is, information on the original construction material, frequency of breakdowns, and the like.

Many cities have only the barest rudiments of knowledge of their capital system. (Peterson, 1980)

Information costs money, precise data even more. The money spent to collect and maintain data is not available for data analysis or for any other of the operations involved in continuous city planning. It is important, therefore, to establish the type, amount, and level of accuracy of the information needed. As implied by the last quotation above, it is usually preferable to have approximate data on time, rather than exact data too late to be utilized effectively. Approximate data may be enough to support many city planning decisions, such as the designation of desirable land uses, highway location, zone changes, and other matters involving many elements, some of which are judgmental in nature rather than quantitatively determined. On the other hand, precision and projective accuracy are needed in population forecasts, most economic and financial determinations, or decisions involving engineering alternatives.

Of course, not all important information is numerical. The attitude of federal, state, and local legislatures toward matters vitally affecting the city are probably better reported by an experienced and broadly informed observer than by informal straw polls, which do not take into account differences in role and political power among legislators. Such important intangibles as the political moods and attitudes of members of the local power structure are probably better read by a knowledgeable and perceptive person informally following a set of prescribed observations, than by attempts at formal scientific opinion sampling. Policies and laws are not formulated as numbers, although they may contain them. Programs of planning effectuation are based more on a general evaluation of conditions, organizations, and public attitudes, than on any scientific study or operations research kind of scheduling. Relatively few critical decisions in city planning are based exclusively on numerical data, mathematical calculation, or scientific survey. "Men can be led by statistics only up to a certain point and then more fundamental values predominate" (Kissinger, 1979).

Correlation

Because each element of a city is directly or indirectly interrelated, correlation is a fundamental part of meaningful planning analysis. By adding another essential dimension of understanding, correlation makes it possible to determine how available resources are best allocated among the primary elements of the municipality, to meet functional requirements for its continued operation, and to achieve certain objectives through progressive change. This allocation of available resources is, of course, the primary purpose of planning. Correlation is therefore part of the analysis necessary to make this assignment. There is almost an infinity of interrelationships among relatively few elements: 3,628,800 among ten elements. Those few elements must be selected that can be treated analytically, and those interrelationships calculated that it is feasible and worthwhile to quantify. Fortunately, continuous city planning requires far more sequential correlations than complete combinational analyses. This not only greatly decreases the number of necessary correlations, but extends the usefulness of the analytical core by avoiding what would oth-

erwise be the prohibitive expense of calculating the combinational interactions of more than very few elements. Also, apart from the factorial
arithmetic involved, the knowledge does not now exist to quantitatively
interrelate the many different kinds of interactions among the primary
urban elements.

Illustrative sequential correlations are shown in the righthand column
of Figure 6, labeled "Correlation Between Categories (Panels)." For example, areal correlations are suggested between population distribution
(A.1) and residential housing (B.9), substandard dwellings (B.10, B.12,
B.15), public and private buses and routes (C.17), unemployment (D.22),
poverty (D.23), industrial production (D.26), water supply system (F.29),
and the sewage/storm drainage system (F.32). These correlations represent well-known relationships between the areal distribution of population and the spatial distribution of several utilities and economic
conditions. While only a few of the many possible correlations are illustrated in Figure 6, they are more than would be maintained by most municipalities. When mechanisms for continuous city planning are first
established, only a few correlations are formally calculated. More are
added as the mechanism is used, the need for additional correlations becomes apparent, and they can be successfully formulated and maintained.

These interconnections are made in various ways: by individual subjective comparison, by group judgments obtained in an organized way, visual comparison of data side by side, by the overlay of information on
transparencies, by ratios developed for comparative purposes and to
monitor change, and by mathematical correlation with or without the aid
of computers. As correlations are used and their validity tested by experience, they are retained, improved, or discarded in a constant process
of analytical advancement.

Because in practice interrelationships are particularly difficult to formulate for comprehensive city planning, quantitatively meaningful interactions are established much more gradually than is sometimes
presumed or pretended. Multiple correlations today are largely personal
and judgmental. After several primary elements or functions have been
interrelated, further quantitative correlation is much more difficult and
most often not attempted at all. Unfortunately, the impression is often
given that city planning conclusions are based on scientifically rigorous
analysis, but in fact they rarely are. It will be some time before this presumed or pretended level of authoritative analysis is attained.

Projection

By definition, projections into the future are an inherent part of planning. Some of these are a matter of choice and are therefore more certain, such as a schedule of construction or a program of expansion or contraction of activities involving no likely constraints. Some projections are the result of previous commitments, such as repayment of bonded debt, municipal contributions to an employee pension fund, or minimum levels of government protection or service. Normally, these kinds of activities and commitments can be reliably projected into the future.

Another category of elements comprises extrapolations from past trends, forecasts based on established correlations, or projections from an accumulation of experience or knowledge concerning the community that are accurate enough for the planning purpose. This category is exemplified by population forecasts and projections of demand for water and energy, municipal tax receipts, or the rate of deterioration of certain physical facilities. Some of these projections—such as forecasting the design capacity of a flood control system from past weather records of local storms—are only partial projections, since they do not forecast *when* the 50- or 100-year "maximum probable" storm will occur again. The reliability of the many kinds of projections in this predictive category varies widely. They require frequent review or continuous monitoring, and a quick response if successive short-range variations from projections indicate a defective forecast or an unanticipated trend.

Each element in the core of analysis is projected separately into the future, in one way or another. If informed opinion or experienced judgment is the best basis available, it is used to make the projection. Sometimes, when a forecast for one element is required in order to project a second element, a best guess is used if this shows the sensitivity of the second or dependent element to the first forecast. The dependent variable can be made more accurate when the forecast for the first element is based on more reliable information rather than best guess.

To the greatest extent possible, all elements are projected together so that they maintain their established interrelationships at each interval of future time. This is by far the most difficult part of planning analysis, possible at present for only a few elements with considerable probable error. Thus, many projections are expressed as upper and lower limits, rather than as one quantity or trend line.

Continuous gathering of information, observation, and analysis are more important than attempts at positive comprehensive long-range prediction. Rather than focusing on the distant future and an end-state plan, continuous city planning starts with today and works toward the future. Of immediate importance are the next several years. Not only is the next fiscal year specifically budgeted, but available funds are always limited by tax rates and assessments, borrowing capacity, state and federal assistance, and other financial factors. What takes place within the next several years will affect what is possible thereafter. It could facilitate the attainment of some city planning purposes, and postpone others or make them impossible. Fortunately, shorter-range projections are normally more accurate than longer-range forecasts.

Continuous city planning first projects the next budget year in detail, the subsequent year in somewhat less detail and certainty, and the following five years as thoroughly as practicable. Every year, this seven-year intermediate span of projection is maintained by adding another year into the future. The first two years constitute an operating plan, integrating the plans of each municipal department for the budget year and the following year with planning for the city as a whole, thereby ensuring that longer-range city plans relate to reality. The projections for the following five years cover the "middle-range bridge," the next most predictable and critical period in the future because it is during this time that successive steps toward planning objectives can be accomplished. Some projections for this five-year period are firm, others are subject to continuous scrutiny and frequent adjustment or revision. (Figure 5)

Projections and plans beyond the intermediate seven-year period of planning are made when they can be reliable enough to justify the time and cost of the projective analysis they require, and when the means for their realization can probably be attained. For example, municipal utility systems involve projections and plans that must usually be started more than ten years before their realization because of the long lead time required for system design, engineering, acquisition of land, funding, approvals, construction, and a test period of operations. The important prerequisite is that these longer-range plans represent firm intentions to produce, and the availability or strong probability of funding and other requirements for effectuation.

Longer-range projections may be employed to evaluate the consequences of alternative courses of action by casting enough light on the future to justify setting longer-range planning objectives now and commencing specific actions to these more distant ends. This kind of projection, or conditional forecast, is analytically the most difficult and most subject to misuse.

If properly employed, . . . conditional forecasts can constitute a valuable tool. The danger lies in the fact that details of the planning process, once the assumptions have been made, are identical in this type of imaginative planning with those that lead to a legitimate program of action [translating decisions that have already been made into the many resulting actions—all interrelated—of departments, groups, and individuals]. . . . It is probably this appearance of reality in the final planning document that accounts for the frequency with which not only the program planners but also members of top management ascribe more validity to the detailed conclusions than the oftentimes highly questionable nature of the assumptions would justify.

Awareness of this danger causes some executives to be less than completely enthusiastic about the formally organized . . . planning process. This is a situation which the practitioners and proponents of . . . planning must remedy. They must take the lead in protecting themselves and others against improper use of projective studies. Every planning document should start with a statement of the assumptions upon which the analysis is based and, when summarizing the results of the analysis, should restate these assumptions clearly as conditions upon the validity of the conclusions.

If the staff planner and the [decision-maker] discipline themselves in this way . . . it is less likely that the planning effort will be carried to unprofitable lengths in terms either of detail or extrapolation into the future: the pyramiding of assumptions necessary to permit such extended analysis will warn the planner when he is approaching the point where what has hitherto been a solid piece of fiction is about to cross the line into meaningless fantasy. (Wooldridge, 1962)

Another set of projections are expressed as policies: stated intentions whose realization depends on decisions and actions taken when the opportunity arises. For example, city planning might recommend that the municipality formally adopt a policy of obtaining more low-income dwelling units when funds are available, when community attitudes are supportive, or when other conditions are favorable. The municipality might decide to allow mobile manufactured homes, the cheapest dwelling units available today, to be located in certain single-family residential zones. Cities might collectively pressure the federal government to subsidize more low-income public housing. Or municipal regulations requiring a percentage of lower-income dwellings in every new subdivision might be adopted or extended and firmly enforced. For the longer-range future beyond the seven-year period of greater planning specificity, there might be a policy of locating low-income housing more widely throughout the community, closer to concentrations of employment, public transportation, or urban "growth centers." Which actions are taken, and in what order, depends on circumstances. If circumstances are unfavorable, implementation of the policy is delayed until developments permit constructive action.

Policies should be more than pious platitudes, serving some purely political or temporarily distractive purpose. They are intended to underlie and shape current decisions and actions. They should be abandoned when no longer relevant. In continuous city planning, policies are maintained as deliberately, conspicuously, and are kept as up to date as numerical material. They are treated as "facts" in different form.

Progressive Development

As indicated, there is a limit to the amount of core information and analysis that can be processed, maintained, and conceptualized for regular reference and decision-making. Many factors are involved: the type of information readily available, its reliability, the time required to revise the analysis or develop alternatives, personnel capable of establishing and maintaining the core analysis, its cost, and limitations of knowledge concerning how different urban elements interrelate. What is attempted in the way of urban analysis and how this is organized and carried out is crucial because city planning decisions and actions are only as sound as the information and analysis on which they are based.

The information maintained and the exact ways of handling it will vary among cities, but there are basic informational requirements (such as some of those shown in Figure 6), which must be met by all successful informational-analytical mechanisms for continuous city planning. Only those data are incorporated that have the requisite reliability, can be updated as frequently as needed, are crucial to the most important matters to be resolved, and are understood and absorbed by the decision-makers.

Above all, additional information and further analysis are incorporated in the core reference only as fast as they can be reliably interrelated with the data and analysis currently considered. At all times, the elements of the core must be meaningfully correlated analytically. More complete information and more comprehensive analysis support better planning only insofar as they meet the fundamental requirement of consistent internal correlation. A very simple construct of information properly correlated is preferable to more material that cannot be interrelated quantitatively or judgmentally. "Model simple, but think complex" is far superior to its opposite. Any method of collection, storage, processing, analysis, and display can be employed that is feasible and meets these basic requirements.

Form

The way analytical material is formulated is important. Delineating the most influential elements of a city and quantifying their interrelationships is no easy task. Every possible simplification or clarification is needed for the planning staff and municipal decision-makers to portray and analyze the functioning of a city.

> [The analytical] craftsman must take into account not only the realities of the decision-making situation but also the characteristic style of the decision-maker. Some public officials will be much more receptive to systematic analysis than others. Individuals differ widely as to how they process information. The types and complexity of the [analytical] structures they use and the ways by which they create, modify, or validate these structures will differ. . . . An analyst who fails to recognize a decision-maker's cognitive style and characteristics risks being ignored. . . . The final judgment on whether decision analysis is useful will, and should, depend on the analyst's craftsmanship in structuring the problem to encompass the decision-maker's central concerns, including the political ones. (Lynn, 1979/80)
>
> One must begin to take seriously the profound mismatches that exist between available analytical tools, the current quality and quantity of theory and supportive data, and what policy makers desperately require and are capable of understanding and utilizing. (Brewer, 1972)

Responsible decision-makers are unwilling to act on the basis of staff analysis that they do not understand. They do not want to act mainly on someone else's say-so, and cannot do so without in effect abrogating their decision-making role to subordinates. When decision-makers are informationally or analytically dependent on other people, they are vulnerable to exaggeration, unrevealed bias, or even deliberate deception. This represents a serious problem confronting executive management generally, as knowledge becomes more compartmentalized, specialized, and mathematical, often requiring computer computation that is understood only by the programmers themselves. Frequently, as pointed out by Dr. Wooldridge in a previous quotation, the underlying assumptions of staff work are often unstated. But decision-makers should not act on studies and recommendations based on assumptions they do not accept. This basic managerial difficulty has not been resolved, and there is as yet no indication of how it might be solved. Until it is, analysis must not be too esoteric, complex, or otherwise incomprehensible for decision-makers to accept and use.

For most people, information in graphic form is more readily comprehended than numbers. As one example, the familiarity of the term "trend line" reflects the conclusion from experience that this graphic expression is the clearest way to present certain information. Superimposing graphics by means of transparencies, or placing them side by side, facilitates comparison. Any spatial separation of interrelated information requires the user to remember one set of data as he refers to another. Memoranda and other written information normally involve remembering material as one turns to related data as close as the next page. An awkward thumbing back and forth with fingers inserted between the pages containing interrelated material or an equally awkward attempt to hold pages in different sections of a document so that they can both be viewed at the same time, is usually necessary. When there are three or more separate pages or other forms of display, the average user will have difficulty maintaining clear enough recall for close correlation.

Of course, forms of analysis should be selected that do not introduce interpretive distortions, such as improperly selected scales for ordinate and abscissa, or presentations of data that imply that small numerical differences are statistically significant. The key criterion of desirable form is whether it makes comprehensive and mental manipulation easier for the planning staff and—more important—for the decision-makers whom they serve. The core of information and analysis for continuous city planning must be directed specifically to the minds and understanding of those who make the final decisions. Otherwise, there can be a serious abrogation of responsibility by those charged with making final decisions, with adverse consequences for democratic society if an elite of computer programmers become the hidden deciders in fact.

Flexibility

Several times earlier in this book, the necessity for city planning to be up to date has been emphasized. Students of the subject have repeatedly observed that city planning in the United States has been ineffective largely because the few components of end-state master city plans that might be acted on are quickly outdated, and it takes ten years on the average to produce a new master city plan. It has also been pointed out that situations develop and events occur that cannot be foreseen and that require immediate revision of existing plans. Being current is essential to successful continuous city planning.

As shown in Figure 6 in the first column, entitled "Recycle," some information needs to be renewed more often than other data. Population and housing, for example, do not normally change so rapidly that they should be resurveyed more than every two years and every year respectively. This does not mean, of course, that population figures should not be updated periodically in accordance with established trends. For some fast-growing municipalities, accurate population data may be needed twice a year if they can be obtained at feasible cost. In the special situation of new towns, week-by-week population figures may be needed because of the critical importance of cash flow. Population increase in the form of new home buyers has been particularly crucial in maintaining the financial viability of the new towns undertaken in the United States by private enterprise with mortgages guaranteed by the federal Department of Housing and Urban Development, but by public authorities in other countries.

By contrast, as indicated also in Figure 6, land-use/zoning information may need to be kept up to date weekly. The dynamics of land-use development in the United States today are such that an unplanned change on a single property can, under certain conditions, trigger a cascade of changes that drastically alter the character of the area from what was intended and formally planned. If at some time in the future planned land-use patterns in cities are more rigorously formulated and observed, land-use data may not need to be brought up to date as frequently.

The other kind of flexibility required in continuous city planning is the capability of revising the core of information and analysis quickly. A natural catastrophe, an emergency situation, or an unexpected decision of major consequence may require immediate revision of this municipal reference. It may be necessary to reformulate the material it contains within a week or a month, depending on the city and the circumstances. Conscientious decision-makers will not tolerate more time lag for revision than is necessary or reasonable.

Both ongoing and emergency reformulation should be borne in mind when determining the process, procedures, and mechanisms of continuous city planning, including flexible displays, as described below. The capability to change quickly is crucial.

The relationship between flexibility and the attainment of planning objectives is conceptualized in Figure 7. Example 1 shows how short-range

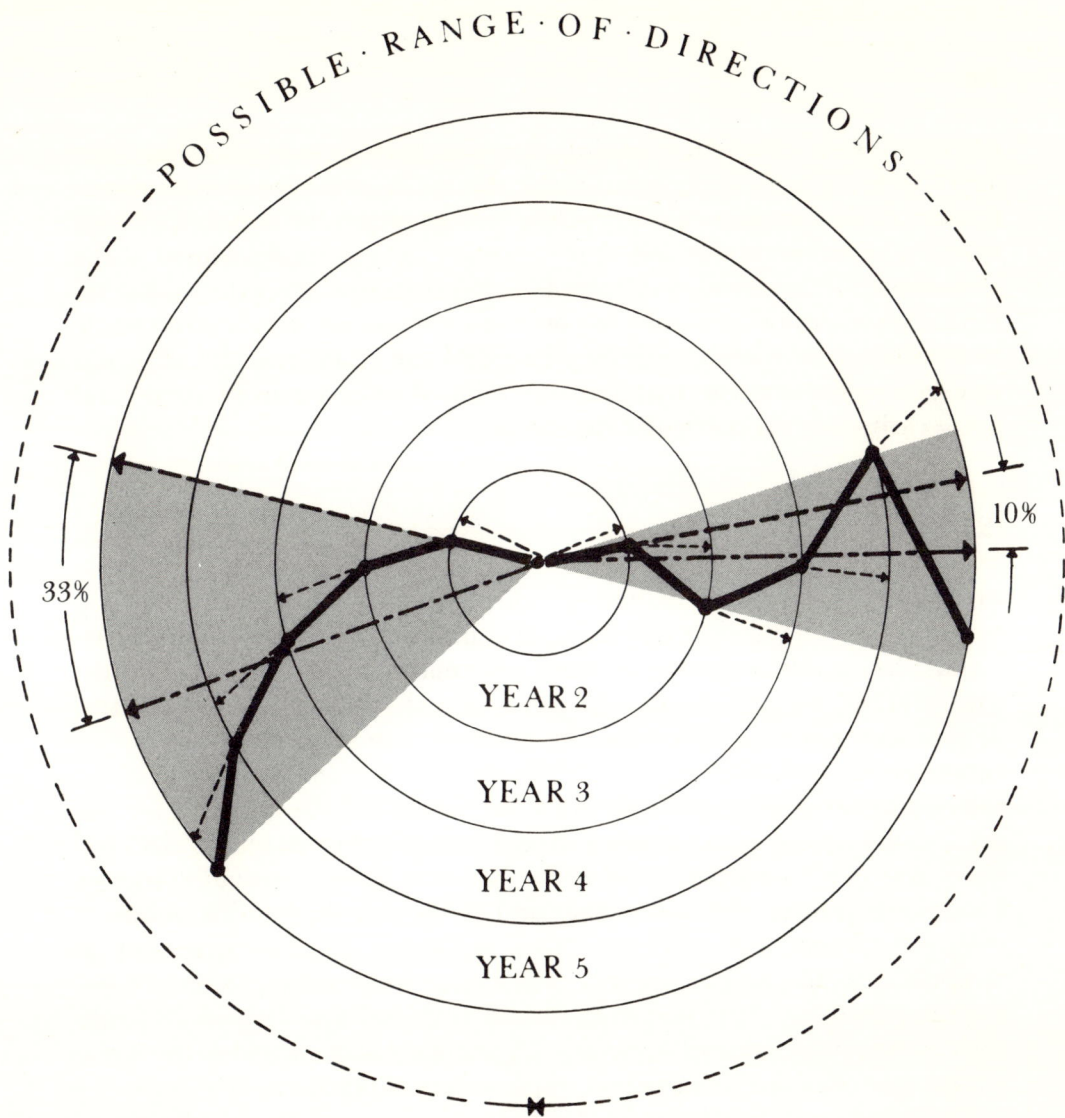

POSSIBLE · RANGE · OF · DIRECTIONS

33%

10%

YEAR 2

YEAR 3

YEAR 4

YEAR 5

EXAMPLE 2   EXAMPLE 1

Direction of Plan Development .... (Annual)

Actual Operating Outcome .... (Annual)

Planned Direction of Development ....(5-Yr. Projection)

Actual Course of Development .... (5-Yr. Period)

%   Variation Between Planned & Actual Development .... (5-Yrs.)

Limits of Variation in Operating Direction .... (5-Yr. Period)

Figure 7   Conceptualized outcomes of continuous city planning.

occurrences can reorient planning each year, first in one direction, then in another. Even though, as shown in the figure, the direction of development of the organism varies each year from what was intended for that year, the outcome at the end of five years is close to that planned at the beginning of this period. In Example 2, the organism has evolved during the five-year period generally as intended (compared with the full circle of possible development indicated), despite the cumulative effect of unforeseen circumstances that have reoriented the organism more and more each year in a particular direction.

DISPLAY

In addition to selecting, gathering, correlating, and otherwise analyzing core data, the method of displaying this information is important. First, it must be readily available to those who make city planning decisions. They will not tolerate the days or weeks it usually takes present-day traditional city planning to respond to an informational or analytical query. City planning commissions have been known to wait literally years before the information they need is developed or found in bureaucratic files. All parts of the core of information and analysis should be available in a matter of minutes for immediate decision, contemplation, or staff study, or for the use of interested individuals and groups, or the general public.

Display panels, such as those shown in Figures 13 and 14, should be as uniform in size and as consistent in format as possible, to reduce the time required for their preparation and revision, and also to facilitate their comparison one with another. A standard size provides the same advantages obtained from similar applications of regularity.

The size of the display panel is limited by the need for it to be transportable by one person from its permanent location in the center for continuous city planning to city council chambers; to the offices of individual lawmakers; to branch administrative centers in certain cities; and elsewhere in the metropolitan region for meetings and reference display. City council members, other government officials, and private groups and individuals may not want or be able to come to the city planning center at all times, but will receive material if it is brought to them.

Displays should therefore be lightweight and small enough to pass through a standard doorway and to fit in the back seat of an ordinary sedan. All things considered, a standard size of 36 by 52 inches is recommended. It may also be desirable to have a number of displays larger in their horizontal dimension; these can be carried through standard door-ways but require a small delivery vehicle if they must be transported any distance. Displays must not be so large that they cannot be easily shifted about within the city planning center described below. They should therefore be as lightweight as possible. Masonite was used for the panels in the planning centers shown in this book, but this material is quite heavy in the size required for display panels. Honeycomb panels are available, which are much lighter, but they may be prohibitively expensive for small communities.

It is essential that displays not be typed, prepared in a drafting room, or printed. The delay inherent in typing and drafting is not fully recognized by most city planners. The preparation and updating of displays in a central drafting pool requires an inordinate time because of exacting handwork, scheduling delays, and remoteness from the deadlines that occur regularly in real municipal life. Printing or even mimeographing studies and specific informational responses takes excessive time under the best of circumstances.

Such delays are unacceptable in continuous city planning, which must permit as prompt revision as feasible. It is highly desirable for staff responses to requests by decision-makers to be available within several hours, rather than days or even weeks later, when relevant information has faded from memory and other matters have come to the fore. To meet this requirement of rapid response, the preparation and revision of analytical displays is done within or next door to the place where they are regularly used. They are not sent out for preparation and processing. They are kept up to date, alternatives are developed, and new displays are formulated *in situ.* In the city planning center shown in Figure 12, analytical material is formulated for the first time, changed, and kept up to date on the display panels mounted vertically in the slides in the wall recesses. When the two main rooms are in use, display boards can be worked on in the small room provided for the storage of panels used infrequently and for reference control.

Another requirement, often overlooked or taken for granted until it is too late, is the design of displays so that they "read" in black-and-white photographs. Color photographs of displays are too expensive for the number of photographic reproductions of core information and analysis needed for legislators, municipal managers, applicants, legal reference, and other purposes. Although most planning staffs are aware of the need to design displays to read and reproduce clearly in black and white, it is surprising how seldom the steps are taken to see that this is done. Much time and money are wasted redoing graphics to correct visual confusion when they are photographed in black and white. This cannot be tolerated in continuous city planning, because maximum conceptual clarity and immediate availability are basic.

Mistakes can be avoided by keeping close at hand a black-and-white photographic reproduction of *colored* graphic materials, to be used as the display is designed and the graphic materials to be used are selected. Since color may be needed sometimes to distinguish visually among different elements of a display that would otherwise be confused, colors should be selected that will be differentiated when the panel is reproduced photographically in black and white. If the display is to be reproduced and printed in color, the printer can indicate the colors that can be differentiated most easily and at least cost.

Figure 8 reproduces portions of several types of flexible display that meet these requirements. They were made to display core information for planning the western activities of a large American corporation, but they are equally useful for city planning.

The following paragraphs correspond to the numbered parts of Figure 8.

1.   *Tabular Chart.*   Portion of a menu-type board covered with felt, preferably black. The name "menu board" derives from the use of these boards in cafeterias to display the menu. Plastic letters and numbers are inserted in continuous horizontal "cuts" or indentations. Elastic cords are stretched to provide linear separations. This type of display can be used for a great variety of statistical material. The numbers and letters in menu-board displays can be changed in a matter of minutes.

This example is part of a panel showing the source and application of funds for a corporation, but the source and application of municipal funds (rarely shown so clearly) could be as readily represented. Part 7 of Figure 8 shows another way of expressing this kind of relationship, with less indication of exact numbers but a much more apparent pictorial correlation of income and outlay by major category.

2.   *Graph.*   The panel is Masonite, with a permanent grid of thin white lines silk-screened on the surface, and covered with a glazed finish sprayed on to allow repeated use of the board. The grid provides a uniform reference scale of two-inch squares, which makes it much easier to align straight lines with stick-on tapes, and in other ways facilitates design and layout directly on the display panels using applied stick-on letters, numbers, and lines (removable tapes). This type of panel is standard

SOURCE AND APPLICATION OF FUNDS

1956	FIRST 6 MOS.		JULY		AUGUST		SEPTEMBER		OCTOBER		NOVEMBER		DECEMBER	
	FRCST.	ACT.	FRCST.	ACT.	FRCST.	ACT.	FRCST.	ACT.	FRCST.	ACT.	FRCST.	ACT.	FRCST.	ACT.
SOURCE														
OPERATING														
NET INCOME		883	165	178	195	240	162	284	206		188		177	
ACCEL. AMORT. RESERVE		0	0	0	0	0	0	0	0		0		0	
DEPRECIATION		283	118	64	80	63	70	73	70		80		80	
CASH INCOME		1 166	283	242	275	303	232	357	276		268		257	

MOVE PLAN

APPROX.

1,000'S OF $	JUNE 30	JULY 31		AUG. 31		SEPT. 30		OCT. 31		NOV. 30	
	ACT.	FRCST.	ACT.	FRCST.	ACT.	FRCST.	ACT.	FRCST.	ACT.	FRCST.	ACT.
ACCOUNTS RECEIVABLE	4 184	4 377	4 556	4 580		6 020		5 390		5 540	
INVENTORIES & OTHER	347	370	439	380		400		470		530	

AVAILABILITY

REQUIREMENTS

PERSONNEL FORECAST

MID-MONTH DATA 12-15-56	1956						1957												1958						SOURCE
	JUL	AUG	SEP	OCT	NOV	DEC	JAN	FEB	MAR	APR	MAY	JUN	JUL	AUG	SEP	OCT	NOV	DEC	JAN	FEB	MAR	APR	MAY	JUN	
EXEC. OFFICE	14	14	14	14	14	14	14	14	14	14	14	14	14	14	14	14	14	14							
A&F CENT. STAFF	162	162	162	162	162	162	162	162	162	162	162	162	163	163	163	164	164	165							RJH
A&F CENT. SERV. 163	358	180	43	43	43	43	43	43	43	43	43	43	43	44	44	45	45	45							RJH
ESS	56	59	61	64	67	69	70	72	74	76	78	79	80	81	82	83	85	87							FSG
GMRD – R–W	756	1074	1145	1095	1150	1208	1255	1300	1331	1362	1394	1428	1463	1498	1519	1542	1568	1582	1597	1612	1619	1626	1634	1640	
NON–SPACE	23	149	173	206	196	205	206	207	208	209	210	211	212	214	216	218	220	222	224	226	227	228	229	230	
MILITARY	423	474	488	509	576	602	627	652	681	710	740	785	830	874	916	958	1000	1023	1046	1070	1088	1107	1126	1158	WCB
OTHER	34	59	26	9	12	12	12	12	12	12	12	22	35	50	36	22	12	12	12	12	12	12	12	22	
GMRD TOTAL	1213	1597	1659	1613	1738	1822	1894	1964	2024	2064	2146	2235	2328	2422	2470	2522	2580	2617	2655	2694	2719	2745	2772	2820	

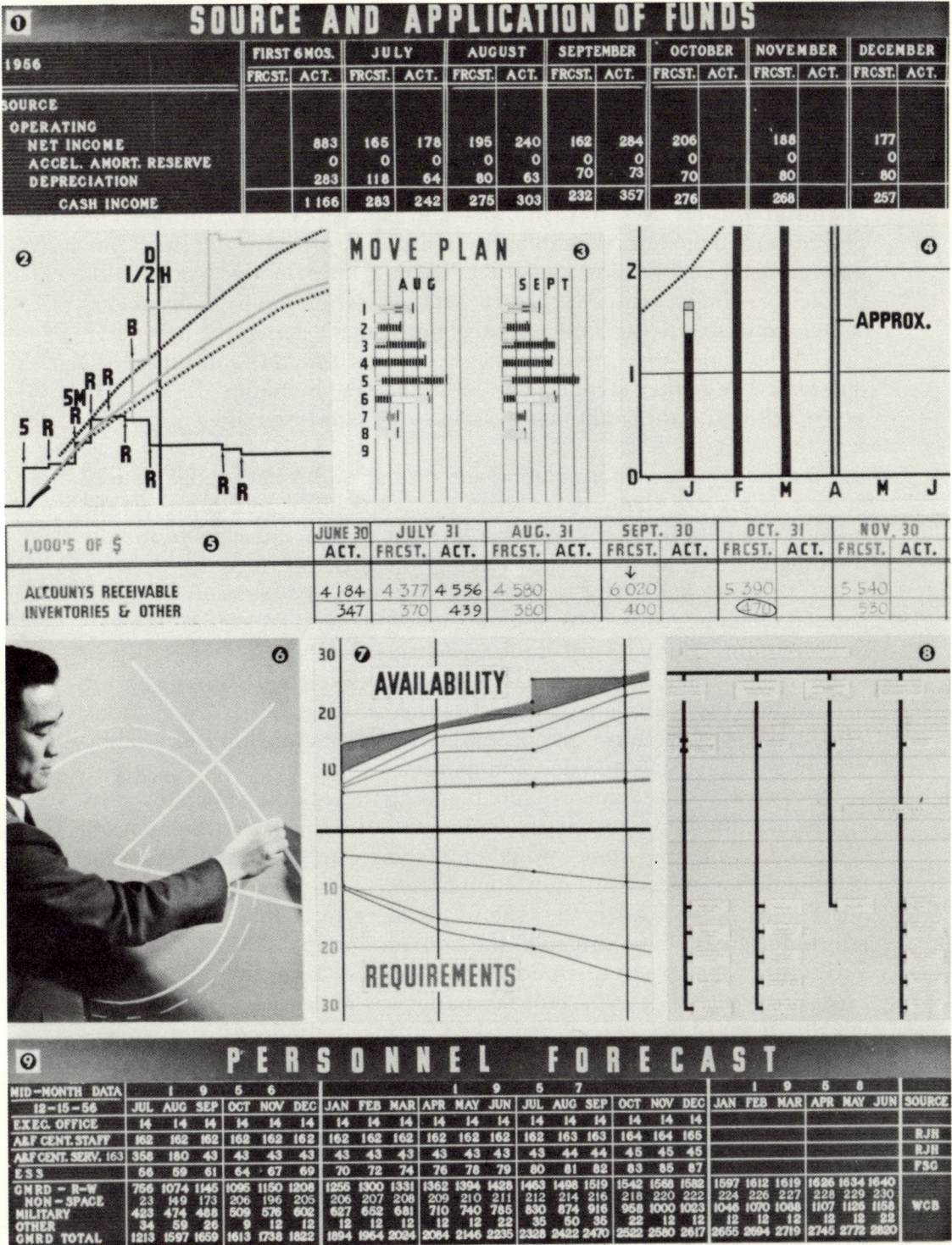

Figure 8 Types of flexible display.

for the many graphic formulations that best express a large part of the analytical information used in continuous city planning. A great variety of types and sizes of stick-on tapes, letters, numbers, and symbols are available commercially.

This graph was used to plan office and laboratory space for new employees in a large and expanding business enterprise. In the small portion of the panel shown, the three sloping lines indicate population projections under three separate sets of assumptions. The darker stepped line, extending approximately horizontally across the lower portion of the panel, displays the capacity of owned (5,5M) and rented (R) quarters. The lighter stepped line indicates new buildings (B, D, ½H), which will house the additional people to be employed after a brief interval of overcrowding.

A more complicated formulation and display of this kind could be used in continuous city planning to depict past experience and to project the relationship between the population forecast for the municipality and the dwelling units required and available to house them.

3.   *Movable Bar Chart.*   The panel is a magnetic metal sheet spray-painted off-white, with stick-on letters and numbers; tapes form the vertical divisions. The bars are cardboard strips with stick-on tapes affixed to the outer visible surface. Small magnets are attached underneath the bars so that they can be rearranged at will on the surface of the panel. This highly flexible form greatly facilitates the examination of alternatives by planning staff and decision-makers.

This panel was used in corporate planning to work out a plan for moving several thousand technical employees among a dozen buildings—some old, some new, some owned, and some rented—of different sizes in different locations. Corporate commitments established an early deadline for the move. This is the type of planning for a program of action referred to by Dr. Wooldridge in the quotation on p. 120.

When the plan was presented to division and department heads, the executives reacted as expected: the move was impossible or would terminally disrupt their unit. When asked, if this was indeed so, to collectively work out a preferable move plan using the movable units representing the number of personnel in each unit, the executives accepted the staff recommendation.

Such a flexible bar chart could be used in continuous city planning to show the composition of the population or the acreage in various zones, or other comparative data for different sections of the city. With movable units representing the principal elements of a proposed planned-unit development, such a flexible formulation could be used to portray and evaluate alternative plans, or to study the best phasing of construction from the viewpoint of the city as a whole.

4. *Bar Chart.* Standard Masonite panel with permanent grid, applied stick-on letters and numbers, and removable tape lines and bars.

5. *Tabular Chart.* Standard Masonite panel with permanent grid and stick-on letters and numbers. Quantities are written with a felt-tipped pen. The surface can be wiped clean immediately with solvent. Informal notations can be made by decision-makers and planning staff, as shown by the arrow and circle.

This kind of display is convenient for analyzing actual and projected city planning data when frequent and easy revision is desired and informal notations are likely to be made in the process. It is midway between a menu board and a blackboard surface.

6. *Blackboard.* As the most immediate and flexible method of graphic expression, the ordinary blackboard should not be overlooked as a means of showing a wide variety of ideas, arrangements, interrelationships, and conditions. These can be expressed pictorially, diagrammatically, numerically, mathematically, statistically, or by other forms of abstract representation and written statement.

Chalk and eraser allow such immediate flexibility that expressions can be developed on the blackboard without appreciable pause, almost as fast as the mind conceives them or discussion develops. Important formulations worked out on the blackboard can be retained by copying them on a display panel, on paper, or photographing them with a Polaroid camera.

7. *Graphic Formulation.* Standard Masonite panel with permanent grid, applied stick-on letters and removable tape, and applied cutout from acetate sheet.

This formulation is another way of depicting and analyzing the availability of and requirements for funds; this information is not now considered in city planning and rarely made available by municipalities in readily understandable form. It is equivalent to the more precise numerical expression of the source and application of funds in Part 1 at the top of Figure 8.

8. *Movable Organization Chart.* Magnetic board using cardboard segments with small magnets attached to their back and typed labels on their front surfaces, and removable tape.

The full panel was used to study alternative ways of formally organizing the components of a corporation, and to display the final version.

The board's metal surface and the small magnets attached to the small cardboard strips allow the cardboard segments to be moved about easily in different organizational arrangements.

This flexible method of analysis could be employed to examine possible organizational arrangements of the continuous planning process within a municipal government composed of numerous departments and agencies as indicated in Figure 2. It could also be used to determine the optimum arrangement for citizen participation so that it supports city planning, and meets federal and state requirements for such participation.

9. *Tabular Chart.* Menu board using plastic numbers and letters, lines made from elastic cord, stick-on letter title.

This type of display panel is ideal for the presentation and analysis of population history, trends, and projections by different categories and in precise numbers. The data can be changed very quickly by simply lifting out the plastic numbers and inserting new ones in the striations provided.

Because population is the basic element in city planning, every municipality should maintain such a board. Public utility, service, and welfare requirements, housing demand, and municipal revenues relate directly to population, as of course do many other economic, social, political, and cultural conditions vitally affecting the city.

REPRESENTATION-SIMULATION

Different kinds of models or "representations of a thing" have long been employed for many purposes including planning. . . . Today, models are used for a variety of analytical purposes. Both small-scale and full-size models are part of the process of designing automobiles, aircraft, ships, and a multitude of simple industrial products. . . . Miniature replicas of all kinds of machinery and equipment are sold commercially for the scale models used by industrial engineers in analyzing alternative layouts for manufacturing plants. . . . For years, prototype sections of highways have been built to full size to test their resistance to the destructive forces of heavy traffic. Flight simulators used to check out commercial airline pilots on emergency procedures . . . are so realistic that the pilots react physically and emotionally as they would under crisis conditions.

Similarly, abstract models have been employed for centuries in intellectual and scientific developments. Mental pictures and concepts constitute simulative abstractions within the human brain. . . . The translation of such mental pictures into symbols on paper constitutes most of the literature of science. An accumulation of thousands of mathematical formulations describe forces, conditions, and interrelationships of matter in physics, chemistry, or biology. . . . Accounting systems are accepted simplifications of the financial operations of a business enterprise. And scientifically selected statistical samples . . . are commonplace in national censuses, opinion surveys, product quality control, and other research directed at a distinct group of people, quantity of objects, or commercial market.

If the concept of simulation is extended further, literature and fine arts may be included, because they seek to describe in their particular way subtle, complex, unquantifiable aspects of the human condition and aesthetic qualities of the human environment. (Branch, 1966)

Since the core of information and analysis provides the simulation necessary for continuous city planning, the municipality must be portrayed in ways that are sufficiently representative of reality to permit meaningful study and sound conclusions. A map shows the ground features of the city at uniform scale and accurate spatial interrelationships. Statistical tabulations depict population characteristics, municipal costs, retail sales, and many other facts and trends numerically descriptive of the city. Instruments measure air, water, and ground pollution in numbers. Descriptive writing may be the best way of expressing certain urban features and development—and it is the only way of stating a planning policy. In each instance, an aspect of the city is being simulated by the most appropriate form of representation or statement.

The physical, spatial, three-dimensional, and visual reality of a city are, of course, essential manifestations of its existence and are root considerations in its planning. It is this physical entity within which the many components of the municipality function. In turn, this spatial entity represents in its anatomy and form the internal forces operating within the city, and external forces exerted by local, regional, state, national, and international situations and activities. The relationship between the physical form of a city and land use, transportation, environment, services, costs, aesthetics, and every other aspect of urban life is now well recognized in the literature of city planning.

What is not widely recognized is the dependence of city planning staffs, commissions, municipal departmental heads, and legislative decision-makers on their personal visual memory to picture the physical city.

All matters which an individual reviews and decides upon are referred to his mind and memory—what might be called his personal internalized simulation, the product of accumulated observations, experience, formal knowledge, and thought . . . The accomplished decision-maker in city planning visualizes a plan picture of the metropolitan region as a whole, as it would appear from an aircraft high above. This internalized view is derived from direct observation on the ground or from the air, from maps and photographs. (Branch, 1966)

However, except possibly in very small communities, a person cannot call to mind a memory image of every part and prospect of a city; there is far too much to be seen and remembered. Certainly, in larger cities and those changing rapidly, the three-dimensional reality is too extensive for one person to survey regularly from the ground. At best, only a fraction of the visual scene can be recalled. Maps assist in this partial recall, but they provide only two-dimensional cartographic information. Even if a city is viewed from a tall building or nearby hilltop, a large proportion of the street pattern and many other physical features are hidden from view by intervening structures and terrain. Of course, much less can be seen standing on the ground at one point or even at several in succession within the built-up area of the city. Every person connected with city planning—commissioners, municipal department heads, and members of the city council—cannot visit every site involved in the many decisions at hand, nor is it practical to provide each of these persons with completely descriptive photographs of every location. As a consequence, city planning in the United States has proceeded half blind.

Aerial photography can provide a picture of the three-dimensional reality of the municipality that can be acquired in no other way, one which is essential for urban analysis and many city planning decisions. Although the photographic view of the city from above is unusual and partial, it is the closest approximation to a complete picturization available. Some features are not shown from directly above because they are beneath an intervening structure or vegetation, are too small to be detected at the photo scale, or are otherwise obscured. Every form of visual and photographic observation is incomplete in some way. Those unfamiliar with aerial vertical photographs must take some time to become familiar with the overhead view, and to learn to read and interpret with ease the large amount of information they contain. Being able to examine aerial stereophotographs through a stereoscope provides additional information because of the three-dimensional view obtained in this way.

Besides containing information, aerial photographs act as triggers to recall to conscious memory scenes in different parts of the city that are stored in every person's mind. If new aerial photographs are taken every six months to a year, this most important visual simulation is kept closely current for continuous city planning, and a record is accumulated that reveals trends and supports a variety of urban studies. Figure 9 shows a standard aerial photographic panel, which is installed in the wall recesses shown in Figure 12.

How a city can be divided for photographic representation on analysis-display boards is shown in Figure 10 for Los Angeles, California. Since Los Angeles covers one of the largest municipal areas of any city in the world, 465 square miles, it is a rigorous test of the feasibility of photo coverage at a scale that permits examining 50-by-100-foot lots, but does not require an impractical number of separate panels.

There are four sets of photographic panels each covering a different ground area at a different scale. One *citywide* photo mosaic covers the entire irregular area of the city shown in white in Figure 10, at a scale of 1 inch equals 4800 feet. This panel is used to view and analyze the entire municipality and such primary elements as its over-all land-use pattern, circulation system, centers of activity and growth, or peripheral developments affecting the city. The seven panels A to G, in Figure 10, which show *sections* of the city at a scale of 1 inch equals 1600 feet, are used for planning that requires examining an area of considerable size that is smaller than the entire city. The twenty-two *district* panels are needed for the many city planning analyses that require the degree of ground detail shown at the scale of 1 inch equals 800 feet and a small enough area to be included on one or two adjacent panels covering 42 square miles each. There are seventy *area* photographic panels at a scale of 1 inch equals 400 feet. Small areas covering only a tiny part of a panel (those crossed with a single diagonal line) are included in free space on adjacent panels. At this scale, individual properties as small as 50 by 100 feet can be studied with reference to requests for zone changes, conditional use permits, planned project developments, and other planning matters requiring detailed examination. The panel shown in Figure 9 is an area panel. A total of 100 panels is needed to portray the 465 square miles of the City of Los Angeles, far more than is required for most cities.

The surface of these standard aerial photographic panels, such as the one shown in Figure 9, is sprayed with a transparent finish to allow tapes and stick-on letters and numbers to be applied and removed repeatedly without damaging the photoemulsion. When a site shown on a panel is under planning consideration, its boundaries can be delineated with thin tape, surrounding zones can be shown with stick-on letter designations, and other information can be noted and called to attention in various ways. A transparent flap highlighting certain facts or features about a

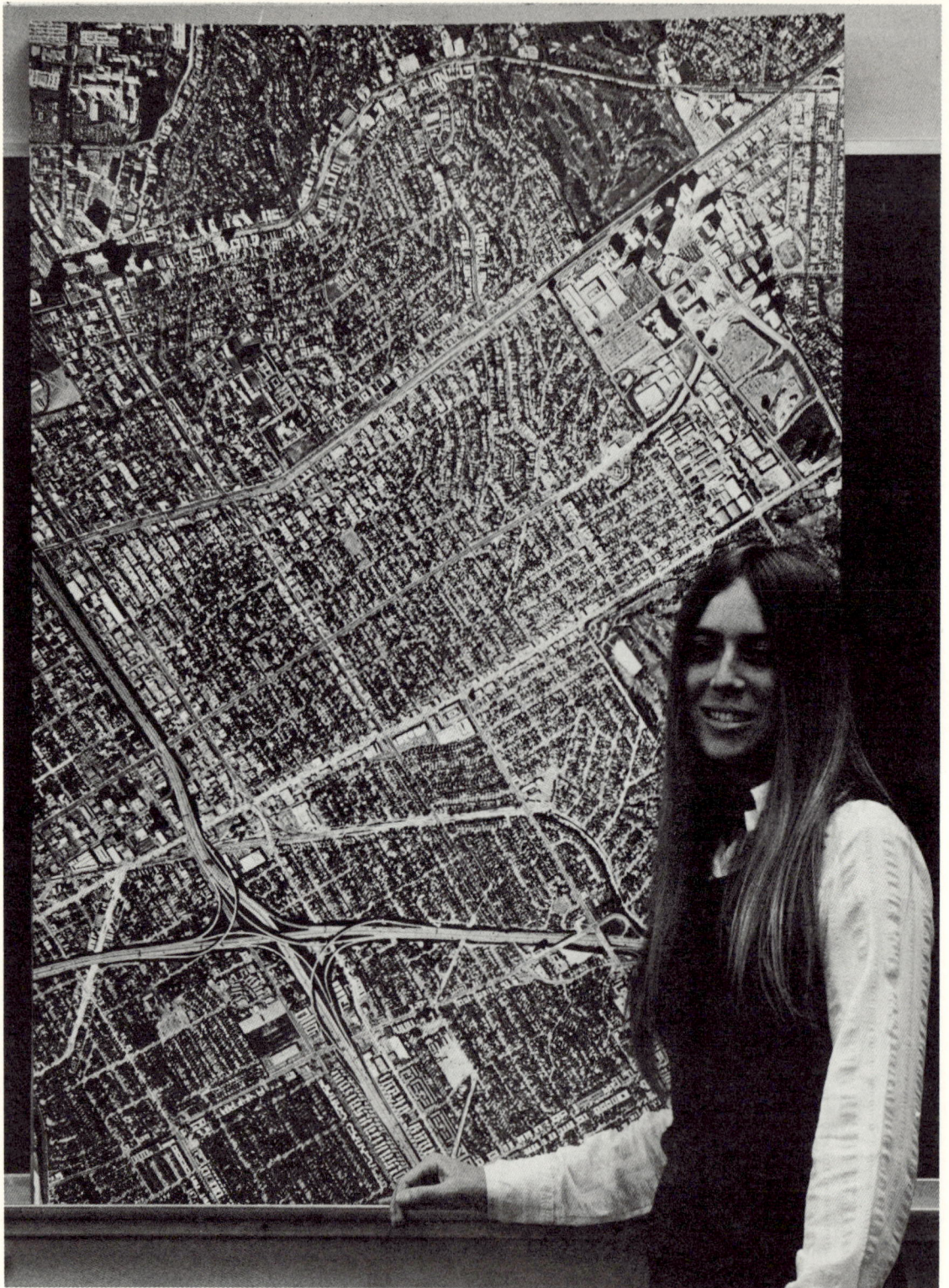

Figure 9 Aerial photographic display panel.

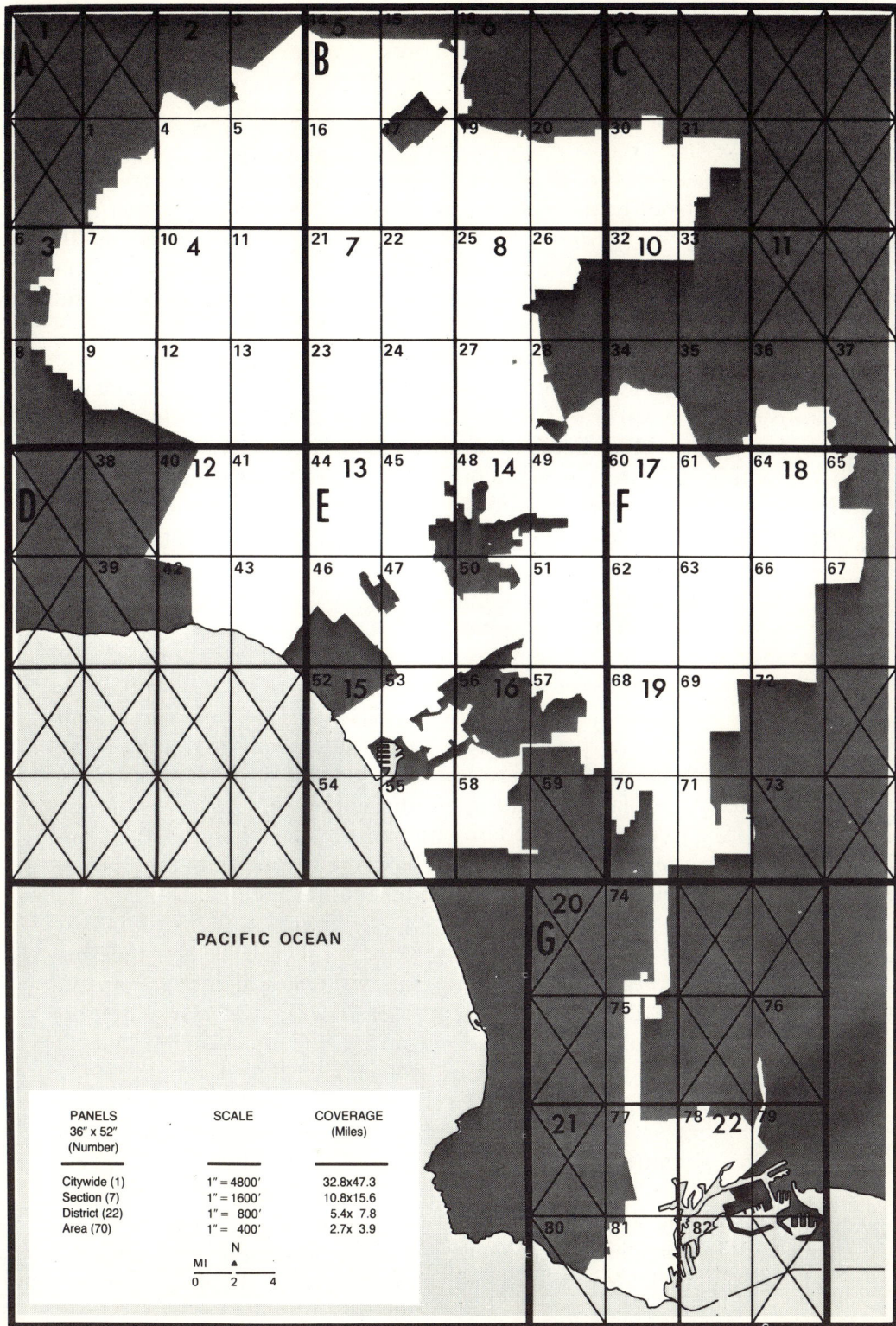

Figure 10 Aerial photographic coverage.

proposed project can be attached to the photographic panel and dropped over the area as it appears in aerial photographic view, the two together showing before-and-after situations. A transparent panel with information affixed to its surface can be slid in front of a photographic panel, allowing the information displayed on both to be viewed and absorbed simultaneously. Other special devices can be developed so that photographic panels serve additional purposes besides portraying the physical city.

Mathematical models have multiplied as a form of simulation since successes achieved by United States scientists during World War II relating to antisubmarine warfare, aircraft bomb loads, and other military strategies and tactics. Most fields of study have applied operations research in attempting to represent mathematically the state of the elements with which they are concerned, and the multitudinous interactions among these elements. Systems engineering, economics, and city planning have undertaken to simulate mathematically the functioning of certain urban subsystems. The aim is to predict such urban dynamics as the amount and location of residential land uses under particular economic circumstances; people's choices among available methods of transportation under different conditions; or the effects of rent control on the many facets of the housing market. Management scientists seek to develop a mathematical model of a corporation that will simulate its functioning so reliably that it can be used to represent the condition and dynamics of the company for most planning and operating decisions. Urban researchers are attempting to formulate a comparable mathematical model, the Community Analysis Model (CAM) referred to in the second quotation below, for comprehensive city planning and municipal management.

Many mathematical models have been used successfully by both business and government for single and several closely related activities susceptible to quantification and meaningful mathematical correlation. But when large complex organisms are considered, with a very large number of elements, many of which are indeterminate or unquantifiable, the reliability of mathematical simulation is so reduced that it should not be used for comprehensive planning. In addition, as pointed out previously, decision-makers are unwilling to commit themselves to mathematical models they do not comprehend.

Perhaps a major failing in our schools of business is the disproportionate emphasis on systematic and complete planning, particularly of a strategic nature. The invalidity of even a single assumption can topple the entire structure with little or no possibility of compensatory salvage. A review of the history of development of successful enterprises would show that the process is largely one of successive approximations which depend on trial-and-error and an opportunistic orientation.

As managers become more aware of the unacceptable assumptions involved in planning models, I would predict a partial swing back to intuition, which actually is often no more than a model too complicated to be precisely specified or verbalized. (Kamen, 1971)

Economics needs to develop models that truly reflect human behavior and to develop data that more accurately measure decision-making factors (Silk, 1977).

Urban model building is a practical art. No urban model contains theoretical formulations of behavior that match the sophistication of papers in economics and other social science journals. First, building an urban model is a massive job. It requires many man-hours of work and the small teams that do the work have neither the time nor the background to become experts on every aspect of background literature. Second, the estimation and computing are limited by the money, time, and capacity available for computing. Third, data are limited, especially on a detailed geographical basis. Thus, it is important not to set excessively high standards for the theoretical foundations of urban models. . . .

Cities are complex systems and an all-purpose urban model is likely to be a no-purpose model. (Mills, 1978)

Simpler mathematical models can be used for simulative purposes in the analytical core for continuous city planning, provided their operation, underlying assumptions, and output are clearly comprehended by those using the calculations. Cost is also an essential consideration. Is a mathematical model necessary to obtain essential information, or can the information be obtained otherwise with less, but still adequate, quantitative accuracy? What are the costs of formulating the model, maintaining it, and producing the printout or other display? In smaller cities, only very limited use of mathematical models will be feasible or desirable, probably in the form of programs with predetermined outputs purchased from another governmental unit or from private enterprise. Computer terminals are included in Figure 12 as part of a model city planning center for a large city.

Mathematical models can be used for limited planning purposes, for example, to simulate the amounts and interactions of the different components of the municipal budget; to maintain an up-to-date inventory of

city land and facts concerning each property, including zoning; or to calculate traffic flow under certain conditions. But a comprehensive model
serving all elements of comprehensive planning, such as the Community
Analysis Model referred to in the quotation immediately above, will not
be available for many years. In the meantime, the kind of overall simulative mechanism and limited mathematic modelling suggested in this
book constitutes the feasible form of continuous city planning potentially
acceptable to urban decision-makers.

If in the future electronic computers are linked directly with the decision-maker, his analytical capabilities might be further improved. For under these conditions he could ask questions of the machine and—provided
answers could be derived from the stored information and calculative programs available in the computer—receive such rapid response that the
mental process is not significantly interrupted. The decider could have before him a television-like display tube which would present information-
analysis from the computer in the graphic form most helpful to him: trend
lines, bar chart, matrix, flow diagram, tabulation, and others [Figure 11,
photo no. 8]. The individual could instruct the computer to modify these
displays to facilitate conceptualization of the material by making it, for example, more or less detailed, changing the grouping of data, or superimposing an array of related information for comparison. In this way,
analytical displays would fit and follow individual thinking. If the person
were also able to "type" into the computer elements of his judgmental
process as he proceeded, there could be recorded immediately for him to
see the sequence of his considerations, the logical accuracy of a series of
interdependent premises and deductions, or perhaps the configuration resulting from spatial postulates expressed in descriptive terms. The computer could thus become in effect an analytical extension of the human mind.
(Branch, 1966)

Figure 11 illustrates a few of the many forms of representation possible. Most of these can be employed in continuous city planning. Exceptions are the centers of the U.S. National Aeronautics and Space
Administration and the Los Angeles Department of Water and Power,
which are for operations control rather than advance planning (photos
nos. 12 and 13). The individual computer consoles shown in photo no.
8 can be used for operations analysis or future planning.

CITY PLANNING CENTER

Information is collected, analysis is conducted, simulations are displayed, and decisions are reached in a spatial mechanism designed for continuous planning. Figure 11 shows two such mechanisms built for different planning purposes, one for a business corporation (photo no. 9), the other for planning and managing the developing of a large military weapons system (photo no. 10). Three of the installations (photos nos. 11, 12, 13) are for operations control more than for longer-range planning purposes.

Figure 12 shows a city planning center as it might be arranged for a large city, but such mechanisms can be developed with the most important basic features in much smaller space and with much simpler analytical displays. In fact, the corporate planning center shown in Figure 11 (photo no. 9) was initially developed and contained on the walls of a single tiny office about 8 by 10 feet. It is the underlying concept and intent, the information maintained, and the analyses made which are important. This can be done in a simple and informal way at first, until the mechanism demonstrates its value and develops into a city planning center.

In the main room of the installation shown in Figure 12, officials, staff planning participants, discussants, and members of the public are surrounded on three sides by walls specially built to contain sliding panels displaying core information and analysis. The recommendatory or decision-making body (city planning commission, planning committee of the city council, city council itself if not too large, or other small group of officials) is on a slightly raised dais at the end of the room, together with several members of the city planning staff and a computer terminal. As shown by the broken lines at the left center of Figure 12, two sections of the analysis-display wall alongside those seated on the slightly raised platform swing out for easier viewing by the audience.

The fixed seats are wide enough or swivel to allow people in the audience to turn to either side and view the side walls more directly. The side aisles are wider than usual to allow small discussion groups to gather in front of analysis-display panels in the side walls. At the end of the room opposite the dais is the projection room from which films or slides are shown on the pull-down screen on the opposite wall. Two of the three public entrances to the room are beside the projection room. Overhead lighting above a dropped ceiling of translucent glass or plastic provides uniform light throughout the room, eliminating shadows cast on analysis-display panels by people standing in front of them.

1.

2.

LAND USE MAPS OF URBAN AREAS

Part of a land use map of New York City, scale 600 feet to the inch. Prepared for the New York City Planning Commission. This map identifies more than twenty different kinds of land use in a very complex urban area. Most of the information shown on this map is based on the Sanborn Map supplemented by special field surveys.

3.

DELMARVA

The darker portions of the map (below and left) indicate areas used by grain farming. The computer prints out such information faster, more accurately, and more cheaply than could possibly be done by a skilled staff working with manual devices.

DELMARVA

Donor: THE CONSERVATION FOUNDATION
Seven months, from August 1, 1966

Staff: CHARLES HARRIS, Associate Professor of Landscape Architecture, Advisor
RAYMOND K. BELKNAP, Research Associate
JOHN G. FURTADO, Research Associate
RICHARD FORSTER, Research Assistant
DUANE BLOSSOM, Research Assistant

4.

7.

5.

6.

FACILITIES PROGRAM

GENERAL FUND EXPENDITURES AND INFLATIONARY IMPACT
1967-68 — 1978-79

142

Figure 11   Forms of representation-simulation.

Graphics

1. Superposition of decibel contours (80–105db) around an outdoor industrial facility on the ground, clarifying the precise environmental impact of various noise sources. (*S/V, Sound and Vibration*, September 1979, front cover)

2. Sample Sanborn map. "Part of a land use map of New York City, scale 600 feet to the inch. Prepared for the New York City Planning Commission. This map identifies more than twenty different kinds of land use in a very complex urban area. Most of the information shown on this map is based on the Sanborn Map supplemented by special field surveys." (*Sanborn Services for City and Regional Planners*, New York, undated, c. 1960)

3. "An Evaluation of Delmarva for Grain Agriculture." "The darker portions of the maps . . . indicate prime land for grain farming. The computer prints out such information in a series of coded numbers and letters. . . ." (*HGSDA Supplement*, Harvard Graduate School of Design Association, March 1967, p. 4)

4. Engraved map-plan, Geneva, Switzerland. An interesting historical example of maps as a long-established but no less important form of representation. (Published by the Society for the Diffusion of Useful Knowledge, London, England, May 1841)

5. Graph: "General Fund Expenditures and Inflationary Impact, 1967–68—1978–79." An example of a clear graphic expression of subject matter in the upper portion of the formulation, and the corresponding numerical quantities in the lower portion. (*City of Beverly Hills, 1978–1979 Budget*, Beverly Hills, California, 1979)

6. Graph: "Facilities Program." Made entirely with flexible materials: stick-on numbers and letters, tapes, and transparent acetate sheet. This graphic simulation was used for several years to plan the construction of new buildings and rental of space to house the projected corporate population. (Ramo-Wooldridge Corporation, Los Angeles, California, 1957)

7. "Econ-o-Rule, Passenger Aircraft." Cardboard slide in acetate sheath. Illustrates in small size (4 by 9½ inches) one of several kinds of special devices which could be produced in a much larger size to permit limited calculations to be made relating to city planning, as part of a standard display panel. (Douglas Aircraft Co., 1956)

8.

9.

10.

13.

12.

11.

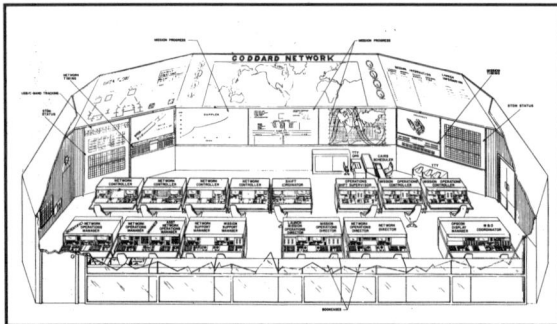

8. Mock-up of a proposed Executive Computer Console, with two display cathode-ray tubes permitting visual comparison of data recalled from computer memory and manipulated by keyboard and light pencil. (Ramo-Wooldridge Corporation, Los Angeles, California, 1957)

9. Planning control room, Ramo-Wooldridge Corporation. Three of the five display locations (four shown in photograph) permit panels to be slid on rollers into view from storage recesses along multiple tracks, separately or superimposed one in front of another. Capacity: twenty standard-size sliding panels ($4\frac{1}{2}$ by 6 feet) and six removable. An overhead view of the model on the conference table is shown in photo no. 18. (Melville C. Branch, "Conceptualization in Business Planning and Decision-Making," *Journal of the American Institute of Planners*, Vol. XXIII, No. 1, Spring 1957, p. 20)

10. Program control room, Guided Missle Research Division, The Ramo-Wooldridge Corporation. "Constructed like a vault to contain Top Secret information, it has reinforced walls, a safe door, and an alarm device. Along both sides of the room are double-tiered display racks in which charts can be stacked, four deep, on recessed holders." (Air Material Command, the Ramo-Wooldridge Corporation, *Control Room Presentation*, Los Angeles, California (Guided Missiles Research Division), undated [circa 1958], p. 11)

11. Integrated work room. "Set up . . . after Boeing engineers found themselves at a technical impasse. On huge sliding panels the status of progress in the critical areas of design . . . is brought into high visibility, for continuous review by SST engineers. . . ." (*Fortune*, October 1968, p. 131)

12. Operations Control Center, Goddard Flight Center, National Aeronautics and Space Administration. ". . . a dimly lit three-story room with 30 computer assisted monitors and large graphic wall displays, some rear projected displaying digitalized information, and with the capability for slides, movies, and live television." [William R. Ewald, Jr., *Graphics for Regional Policy Making, a preliminary Study*, Washington, D.C. (for the National Science Foundation), 17 August 1973, pp. 17–19]

13. Load dispatching center, Los Angeles Department of Water and Power. Being replaced by an energy control center making greater use of electronic computers and automatic dispatch devices. The center shown is a closer analogy to a mechanism for continuous city planning because it does not include electronics which are overautomated for the municipal planning mechanism explained in this book.

Figure 11 *(Continued)*

14.

15.

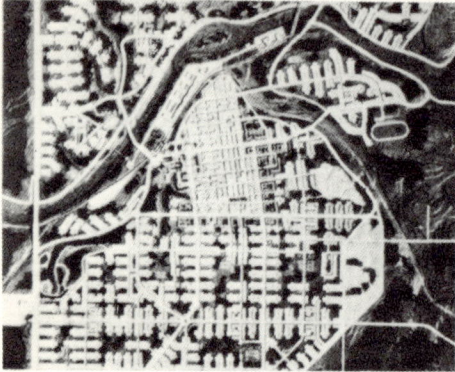

16.

19.

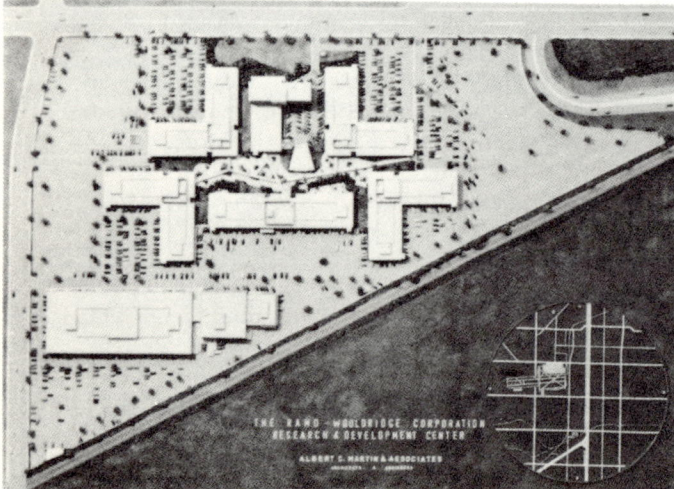

18.

THE RAND-WOOLDRIDGE CORPORATION
RESEARCH & DEVELOPMENT CENTER

ALBERT C. MARTIN & ASSOCIATES

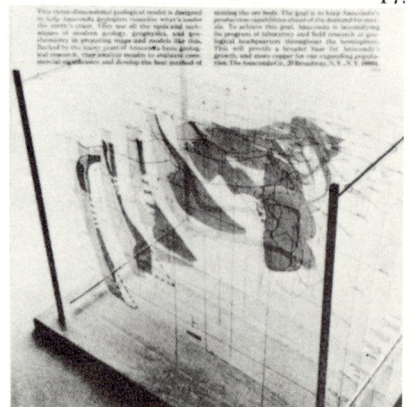

17.

146

14. Scale model, Inland Sea of Japan. "Government-financed hydraulic model—an 8970-square-yard (7176-square-meter) scale reproduction. . . . Simulated tidal currents carry red dye . . . representing the spread of effluents from industrial and urban areas." The figure crouching in the middle lefthand portion of the picture indicates the large size of the simulative model. (Source unknown)

15. Scale model of city, Diorama, General Motors Building, New York World's Fair, 1939. Part of an installation covering 35,000 square feet (3150 square meters) within the General Motors building. Called the Futurama, the models depicted the American countryside as it might appear at the turn of the next century. Models of this type (rather than working models for planning purposes) have been used for descriptive display in Hannover, West Germany; Stockholm, Sweden, and Philadelphia in the United States.

16. Industrial production planning model. "Every phase of the material-handling problems and the traffic they create within the plant and within the surrounding yard area can be quickly and accurately solved" using exact scale models of processing and incidental equipment. "One of the great advantages of the . . . layout is its complete flexibility." ("Visual" Planning Equipment Co., undated, c. 1949.)

17. Geological model. "This three-dimensional geological model is designed to help Anaconda geologists visualize what is under the earth's crust." An example of a physical model specifically formulated to portray a spatial configuration otherwise difficult of impossible to conceptualize. (The Anaconda Company)

18. Scale model, research and development center. A finely finished scale model of a complex of buildings constructed in Hawthorne, California, to house 5000 employees, built by a professional modelmaker from final architectural plans and specifications. Used for reference, display, public relations, and other corporate purposes. (The Ramo-Wooldridge Corporation, 1957)

19. Working model of a new town. Base constructed of cardboard layers for each contour level. Initial study used removable tapes for streets, and movable buildings made of balsa wood. (Cranbrook Academy of Art, Bloomfield Hills, Michigan)

Figure 11 *(Continued)*

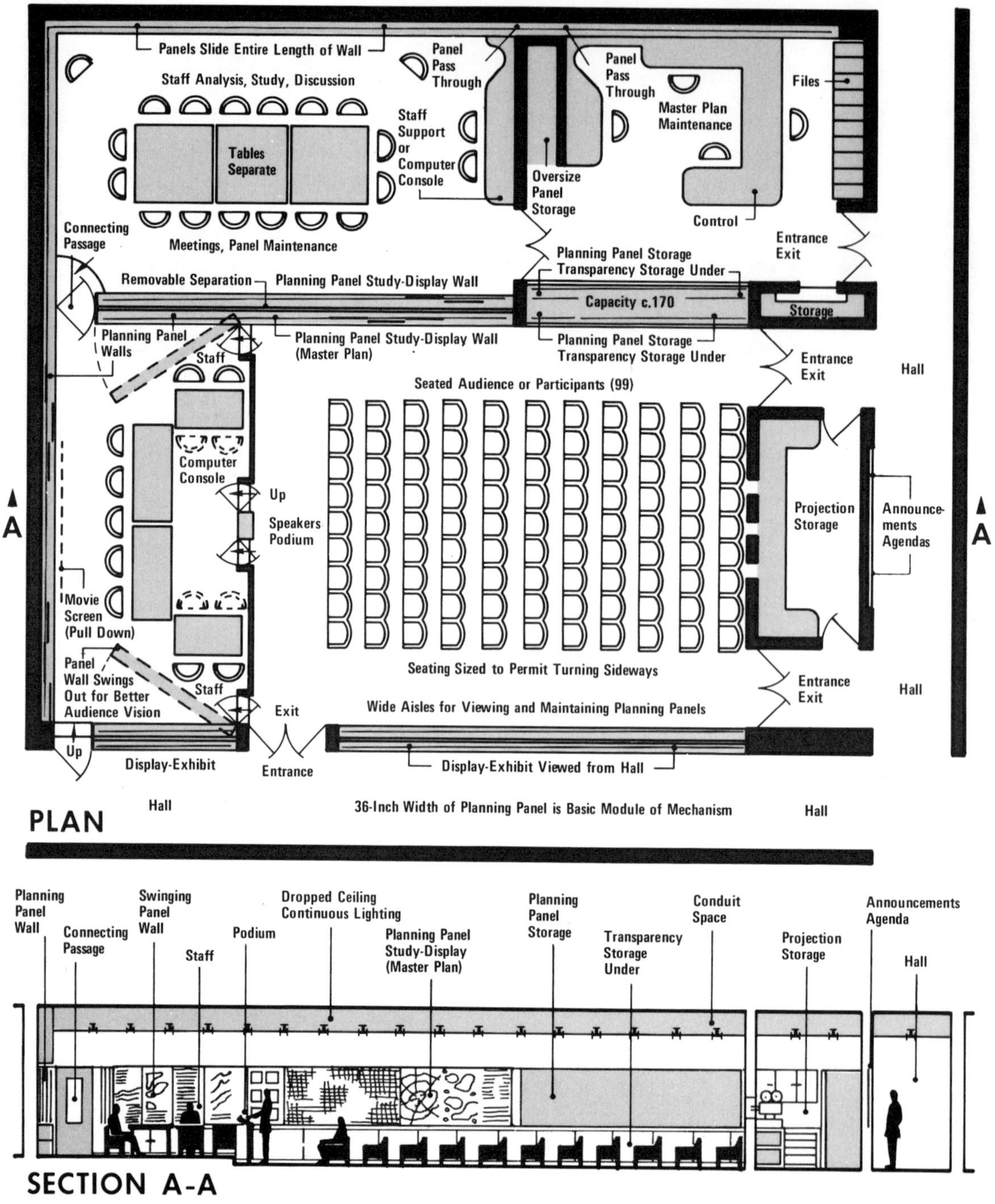

PLAN

- Panels Slide Entire Length of Wall
- Staff Analysis, Study, Discussion
- Tables Separate
- Connecting Passage
- Meetings, Panel Maintenance
- Panel Pass Through
- Panel Pass Through
- Staff Support or Computer Console
- Master Plan Maintenance
- Files
- Oversize Panel Storage
- Control
- Entrance Exit
- Removable Separation
- Planning Panel Study-Display Wall
- Planning Panel Storage Transparency Storage Under
- Capacity c.170
- Storage
- Planning Panel Walls
- Staff
- Planning Panel Study-Display Wall (Master Plan)
- Planning Panel Storage Transparency Storage Under
- Entrance Exit
- Hall
- Seated Audience or Participants (99)
- Computer Console
- Up
- Speakers Podium
- Projection Storage
- Announcements Agendas
- Movie Screen (Pull Down)
- Panel Wall Swings Out for Better Audience Vision
- Staff
- Exit
- Seating Sized to Permit Turning Sideways
- Entrance Exit
- Hall
- Up
- Display-Exhibit
- Entrance
- Wide Aisles for Viewing and Maintaining Planning Panels
- Display-Exhibit Viewed from Hall
- Hall
- 36-Inch Width of Planning Panel is Basic Module of Mechanism
- Hall

SECTION A-A

- Planning Panel Wall
- Connecting Passage
- Swinging Panel Wall
- Staff
- Podium
- Dropped Ceiling Continuous Lighting
- Planning Panel Study-Display (Master Plan)
- Planning Panel Storage
- Transparency Storage Under
- Conduit Space
- Projection Storage
- Announcements Agenda
- Hall

Figure 12 City planning center.

148

Connected with this main room by a door at the rear of the dais is an adjacent room for staff support and meetings of many kinds. Here, as well as in the main room when it is not being used for a formal purpose, the core of information and analysis is developed and maintained directly on the display panels by the planning staff. Here, staff groups large and small meet, and professional people from other units of the municipal government, representatives from other agencies and organizations, or visitors from abroad gather for explanatory sessions and discursive meetings. Members of the city council, municipal department heads, or advisory groups use this room for working sessions preliminary to formal meetings or hearings held in the main chamber. In the staff room, studies can be made or reviewed that are merely exploratory, and should not be seen and construed by the public as final resolutions, definite proposals, or possible alternatives. To this extent, the staff room serves as staff study space with restricted access.

Three of the four walls of this room contain display panels. Since the tracks on which the panels roll are continuous along the end walls of both staff and main rooms, display panels can be rolled directly between these two rooms, as shown in Figure 12. Similarly, display panels can be rolled directly back and forth along the wall between the staff room and the adjacent record-control room, through the opening marked "panel pass through" in Figure 12. There is a second computer terminal and visual display in the staff room.

Connected with the staff study space is a third smaller space, a record-control room specifically designed for collecting and keeping track of the information and analysis maintained on the display panels. Here, desks and files are arranged to facilitate work directly on a display panel which cannot conveniently be formulated or revised when it is installed in one of the other two rooms. By making and maintaining the displays directly on the panels in the wall spaces built to contain them, the inevitable delays, inflexibility, and higher costs of transporting the panels back and forth between the city planning center and a conventional drafting room are avoided. Direct production and maintenance of the panels reflects and reinforces the continuous, up-to-date nature of the analysis, and utilizes departmental plans and proposals and other information flowing to and from the city planning center.

In the record-control room, the photographs of the display-analysis panels taken regularly are filed as the official, legal record of the master city plan they constitute, as it develops and changes. There is also space provided for the storage of panels larger than the standard dimensions, and those used so infrequently that they should not take up space in the display walls.

It will be noted in examining Figure 12 that provision for analysis-display panels is made throughout the installation, in all but several short walls. Display walls contain six to eight tracks at the top and bottom of recesses, with regularly spaced rollers making it easy to slide panels into view one from behind another, or to slide transparent panels in front of photographic and other display boards. Panels may also be placed side by side in the same or separate tracks. Many such groupings and super-positioning of analysis-display panels are possible without moving them to different tracks, but the wall recesses are designed so that the panels can also be shifted easily from one track to another.

The wall recesses on both sides of the main room are designed so that panels can be put in place and removed by a person standing on either side of the wall. Thus, planning staff can change the display panels while standing in the staff room facing the auditorium seats in the main room, or while standing in the main room facing the staff room. Or one can reach through the wall and reverse panels that have been used in the main room so that they face the staff room permitting reference and study from this space. Similarly, panels can be shifted freely in the opposite wall between the main room and the adjoining corridor. In this way, some analysis-display panels may be faced toward the corridor so that participants and spectators have the opportunity to review material concerning city planning matters coming up for hearings, discussion, or decision. Or the wall as seen from the corridor can contain regularly replaced panels displaying elements of the master city plan for anyone interested.

At least 300 standard-size panels can be displayed and stored in the installation illustrated in Figure 12. If ease of rearrangement in the wall recesses is sacrificed by filling them to capacity, approximately twice the number of panels can be accommodated. Two hundred and twenty-four panels would probably be the maximum number needed to conduct continuous city planning for a city the size of Los Angeles. Smaller communities would not only have more modest city planning centers, but far fewer analysis-display panels as well.

Analysis-display panels are of two basic types: opaque and transparent. When the latter are rolled in front of other panels, they provide direct comparison of information by visual superposition. Provided what is shown on one transparent panel does not obscure or confuse what is displayed on panels behind, as many as four transparent panels may be correlated in this way.

Many different types of opaque displays are shown in Figure 8. The analytical potential of continuous city planning display is illustrated by Figures 13 and 14. A Planned Financial Program is admirably conceived analytically and graphically in Figure 13 (without the text added to the graphs for publication in a master plan booklet). Although the numerical quantities and interrelationships could be stated mathematically, it would be impossible without a graphical expression for anyone other than a mathematician to comprehend so complicated a financial program covering five years. On such a crucial matter as financial plans for the city's future, municipal decision-makers would certainly not act on the basis of mathematical equations and calculations they do not undersand. Nor would other persons concerned and the public at large understand such a mathematical statement of a financial plan. In the second example (Figure 14), essential personnel (population) data are maintained on a menu board, in this case for a corporation. It could as readily be maintained for a city, for the data are easy to comprehend and the display can be revised quickly to incorporate population changes.

Figure 12 shows locations for computer consoles in both main and staff rooms. As more information can be absorbed, analyzed, and utilized effectively by those directly involved in city planning, computers may be used for data storage, retrieval, processing, calculation, and display on large screens. The entire mechanism depicted in Figure 12 may be operated by computers and electronic display devices some time in the future.

The efforts of computer scientists and businesses selling computer hardware and software to upgrade municipal decision-making have been successful in certain limited, functional operations, but they have been notably unsuccessful with respect to comprehensive city planning. In the main, this is because of a lack of understanding of the nature and complexity of cities, of governance in a democracy, and of the capabilities, limitations, and responsibilities of human decision-makers in the real world of urban government. The mechanism described here represents the next advance in municipal government management and planning. However, as discussed later, it will be difficult to achieve, even over an extended period of time. (Rout, 1980)

Detailed consideration of the construction and functioning of the city planning center should never obscure its basic purpose of providing city

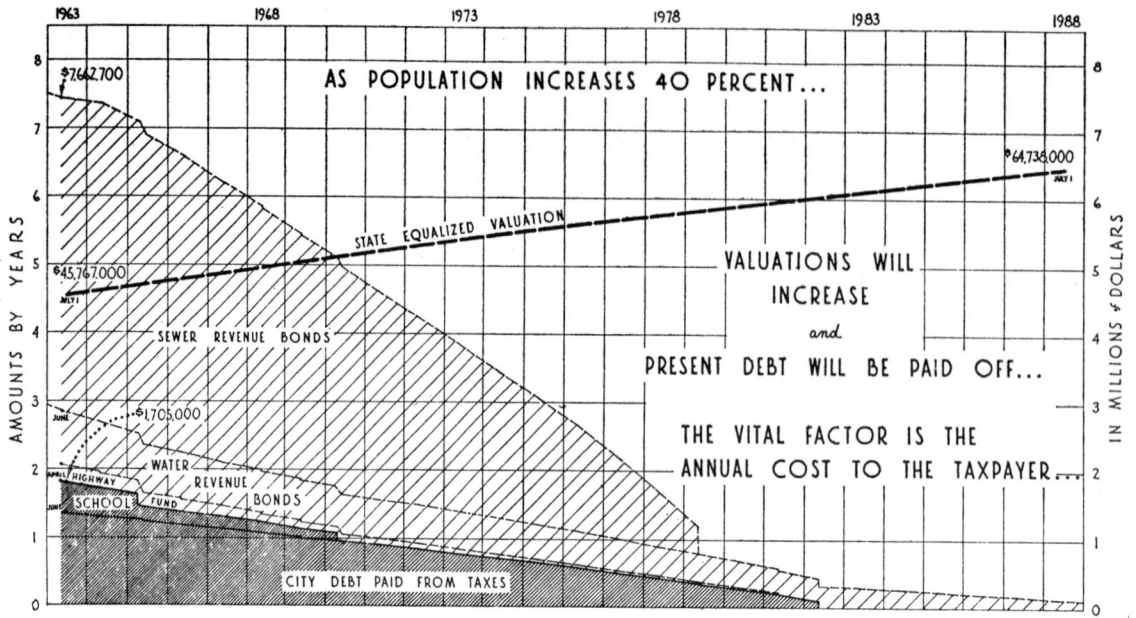

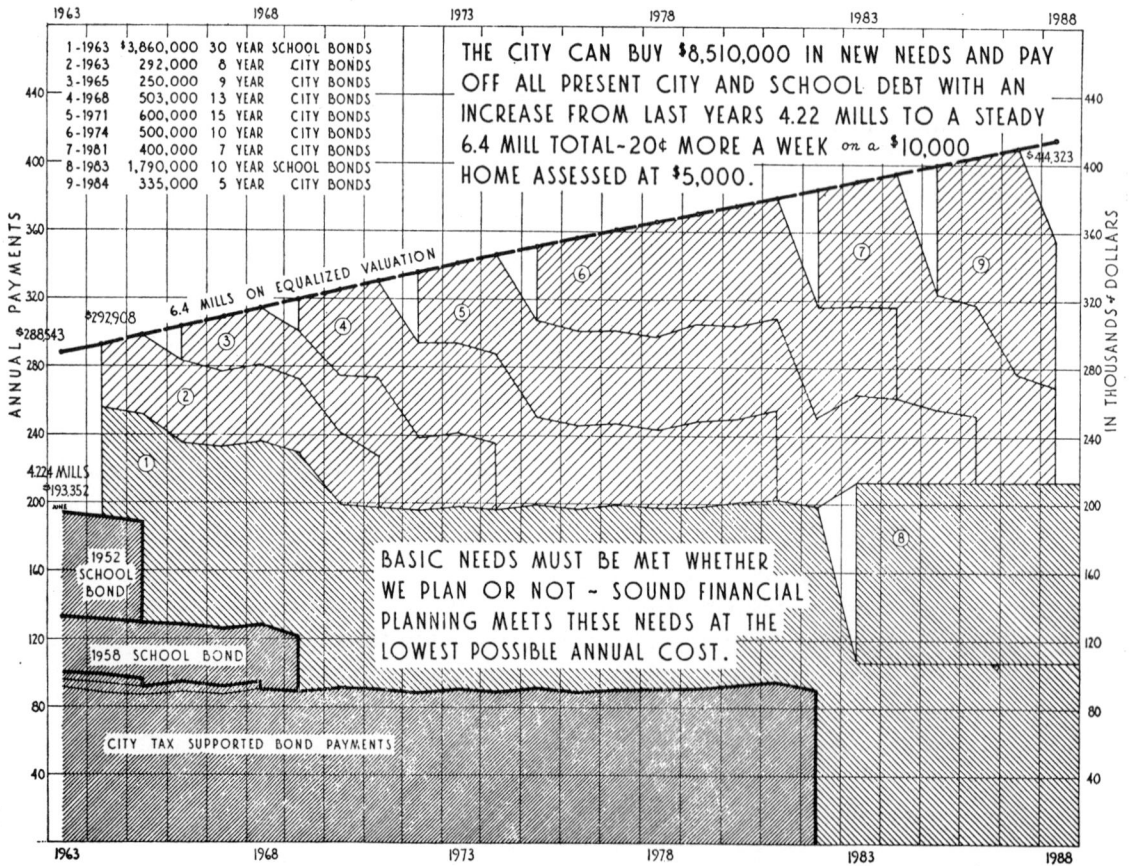

Figure 13 Illustrative analysis-display panel (a planned financial program).

P E R S O N N E L   F O R E C A S T

MID-MONTH DATA 4-1-57	JAN	FEB	MAR	APR	MAY	JUN	JUL	AUG	SEP	OCT	NOV	DEC	1ST MID-QTR	2ND MID-QTR	3RD MID-QTR	4TH MID-QTR	SOURCE
EX.EC. OFFICE	14	14	14	17	17	17	18	18	18	18	19	19	20	20	20	20	
A&F CENT. ADMIN.	162	162	162	212	218	223	227	231	236	241	246	251	268	272	276	280	RJH
CENTRAL STAFF	43	43	43	38	40	42	44	46	48	50	52	54	61	67	70	75	RJH FSG
GMRD - R-W	1255	1300	1331	1350	1395	1447	1479	1510	1542	1575	1607	1625	1663	1713	1733	1733	
NON-SPACE	206	207	208	255	259	265	265	266	267	267	268	268	270	271	273	273	
MILITARY	627	652	681	767	812	858	877	897	914	931	948	961	989	1022	1060	1090	WCB
OTHER	12	12	12	24	24	24	50	50	35	24	24	24	24	24	50	24	
GMRD TOTAL	1894	1964	2024	2141	2231	2329	2406	2457	2491	2530	2579	2610	2676	2759	2843	2847	
COMMUNICATIONS	483	544	573	540	568	595	605	610	616	625	630	636	650	660	661	665	RJVN
NON-SPACE	55	55	56	51	51	52	55	57	57	58	58	59	63	65	65	68	
SPEC. MANUF.	98	98	98	125	127	129	131	132	133	138	140	142	143	144	145	145	
COMPUTER CENTER NO. 1	318	328	341	340	352	373	394	416	444	455	466	476	486	496	506	516	RJB
CENTER NO. 2	107	110	118	126	134	142	150	160	110	110	110	110	110	110	110	110	
NON-SPACE									50	50	50	50	55	55	55	55	
SPEC. MANUF.									18	19	20	20	21	21	22	22	
CONTROL	245	250	253	338	369	396	406	418	426	434	442	447	478	510	541	547	MVV
NON-SPACE	30	30	30	25	26	26	29	30	31	32	33	34	39	45	48	54	
SPEC. MANUF.																	
A R L	28	31	33	31	33	37	38	39	40	40	41	42	44	46	55	55	DF
NON-SPACE																	
E R L	24	26	27	22	24	25	27	28	30	32	33	35	39	43	47	51	FSG
NON-SPACE																	
ELECT. INSTR.	125	134	143	170	170	170	136	136	136	136	136	136	136	136	136	136	GF
NON-SPACE																	
SPEC. MANUF.	20	22	24	50	50	50	50	50	50	50	50	50	50	50	50	50	
INFO. SYSTEMS				14	16	19	22	24	27	30	32	34	38	42	46	50	RPJ
OTHER				-	1	9	23	23	3	-	-	-	-	11	27	-	
R-W L.A. TOTAL	2767	2904	2994	3072	3202	3344	3396	3476	3563	3636	3704	3755	3883	4005	4091	4128	
NON-SPACE	291	292	294	331	336	343	349	353	373	376	379	381	393	402	408	417	
L.A. TOTAL OTHER	639	664	693	791	837	891	950	970	952	955	972	985	1013	1057	1137	1114	
MIL.	627	652	681	767	812	858	877	897	914	931	948	961	989	1022	1060	1090	
NON-SPACE																	
OTHER	12	12	12	24	25	33	73	73	38	24	24	24	24	35	77	24	
TOTAL OUTSIDE L.A.	90	99	108	100	107	114	158	162	170	176	182	188	211	254	298	339	
MIL. REQ.	6	6	6	7	7	7	7	7	7	7	7	7	7	7	7	7	
DENVER R-W OTHER	10	15	20	16	18	20	60	62	66	70	75	80	100	140	180	220	
BOSTON R-W OTHER	12	15	18	15	19	23	26	28	30	32	33	34	37	40	44	45	
FIELD-GMRD OTHER	62	63	64	62	63	64	65	66	67	67	67	67	67	67	67	67	
GRD. TOTAL R-W	2857	3003	3102	3172	3309	3458	3554	3638	3733	3812	3886	3943	4094	4259	4389	4467	
ACTUALS	2710	2840	2966														
GRD. TOTAL OTHER	639	664	693	791	837	891	950	970	952	955	972	985	1013	1057	1137	1114	
ACTUALS	572	617															
	JAN	FEB	MAR	APR	MAY	JUN	JUL	AUG	SEP	OCT	NOV	DEC	1ST QTR	2ND QTR	3RD QTR	4TH QTR	

Figure 14   Illustrative analysis-display panel (personnel forecast).

planning staff and municipal decision-makers with information and analysis that are affordable, that will be used regularly, and that improve the quality of planning decisions. The precise nature and size of the center will vary, depending on a community's size, stage of development, form of municipal government, local power structure, and the personalities of the people in the most influential positions.

If need be, the planning center for a very small community can be maintained in a tiny office, with flexible materials on cardboard panels displaying only the most basic information and requiring none of the special installation suggested for larger cities. Successful continuous city planning depends on the nature rather than the elaborateness of the mechanism employed for its application. The basic requirements of information collection, urban analysis, decision-making, and implementation remain the same.

The city planning center should be located as close to the seat of municipal government decision-making as possible. Since the center is intended to be used regularly by legislators, department heads, and the many professional persons participating in city planning, accessibility is clearly important. Ideally, the center should be the place where these people can stop by regularly to review current information and analysis; obtain and contribute specific information; attend informal work sessions, staff meetings, public hearings, and presentations; or take part in formal decision-making.

The need for such a mechanism has been well expressed with reference to the Situation Room in the White House. Here, in an installation physically different from a city planning center but serving a comparable purpose, information and analysis are maintained to provide background for discussions and decisions relating to foreign policy and other important national security issues. Such installations exist in the Pentagon and other centers of military decision, supporting their different requirements.

There exists no regular staff procedure for arriving at decisions; instead, *ad hoc* groups are formed as the need arises. No staff agency to monitor the carrying out of decisions is available. There is no focal point for long-range planning on an inter-agency basis. Without a central administrative focus, foreign policy turns into a series of unrelated decisions—crisis oriented, *ad hoc* and after-the-fact in nature. We become the prisoner of events. (Nelson Rockefeller, in Kissinger, 1979)

The risk of rash decisions lies . . . in *ad hoc* meetings in the Oval Office, the Cabinet Room, or the personal offices of Cabinet members. There the danger is real that plausibility is confused with truth and verbal fluency overwhelms cool analysis. It is there that in the absence of staff work, decisions may be made which the facts do not support, where individuals talk to impress and not to elucidate at a time when precision is crucial. The temptation there is much greater than in the Situation Room to allow a fleeting and superficial consensus to ratify unexamined assumptions. There are the simultaneous risks of paralysis and recklessness. Principals cannot really know the consequences of their recommendations unless those recommendations have been translated into specific operational terms. (Kissinger, 1979)

The city planning center is a mechanism for *planning,* not for operations control. Many installations are developed to monitor ongoing operations and to facilitate quick restoration of equilibrium when normal conditions have been disturbed by unforeseen events. Hundreds of industrial and commercial establishments have such operations-control centers. The military have elaborate centers for the command and control of aircraft carrier operations, the intercontinental ballistic missile system, strategic air command, and the nuclear submarine force. Years ago, two of these were conceptual precedents for the city planning center described in this book, except that one of them was designed for command control of *operations* rather than *planning.* (Figure 15)

There have been very few centers designed for comprehensive planning. While such planning centers must maintain up-to-date information on operations if plans are to reflect current reality, their purpose is to provide staff support for planning ahead. Operations control is left to the line or producing units; they can or should be able to do this better than anyone else, since monitoring and controlling their own operations is essential to their success. Also, overcentralization of operational control, whether deliberate or inadvertent, produces administrative rigor mortis at the top level of management and command.

There is a built-in tendency for staff planning centers to collect more information, and gradually to assume more and more directive prerogatives. If this occurs, the center becomes a place for monitoring and managing current operations rather than for planning. This tendency to acquire line responsibilities is in part because planning staffs spend their time studying and analyzing; they are free from daily and even hourly executive or supervisory demands, which take so much of the time and attention of line managers. Thus, the staff planner's knowledge appears

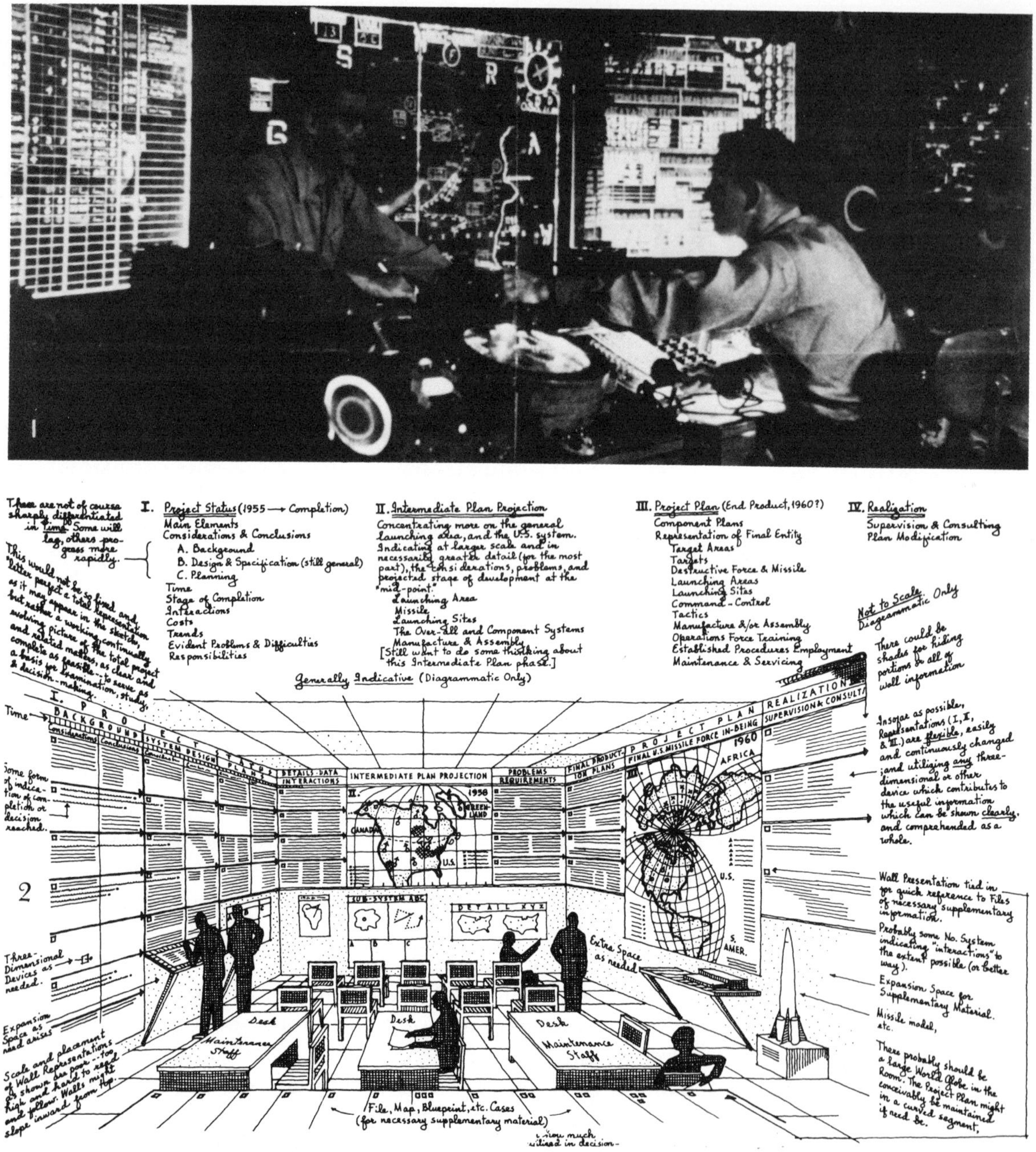

Figure 15 Conceptual precedents from the military world.

1. "The eerily lighted cavern . . . on the U.S.S. Lake Champlain . . . is a fantastic brain which guides the fighting of a modern aircraft carrier. Called the Combat Information Center, it is the most complicated feature aboard a craft spectacularly complicated anyway, a restless airfield of 890 feet and 83,100 tons with a crew of 3,366 who must launch 600-mph planes and defend the ship against enemy planes of like speed. CIC collects for split-second action all information on the ship's combat readiness. . . . The CIC brain never stops thinking, watching. . . ." (*Life*, Vol. 35, 28 September 1953, p. 70)

2. "To be effective, planning must . . . provide a *useful* & *used* 'working tool' for study, design, and decision-making . . . an integrative and projective 'view' of continuous day-to-day importance . . . rather than some form of 'dream' effort more or less unrelated to current operations and the real problems of the moment. . . ." [Melville C. Branch, Jr., "Speculations on Some Aspects of Planning a U.S. Intercontinental Ballistic Missile Force," Los Angeles, California (Ramo-Wooldridge Corporation), December 1954, mimeographed]. See also: Figure 11, illustration 10, for the representation-simulation stimulated by this proposed "working tool."

Figure 15 *(Continued)*

exaggerated to those who can spend much less uninterrupted time on analysis and planning. Staff planners are competent people whose capabilities may therefore appear relatively greater than they are in fact, all the more so since staff planners tend to exaggerate their comprehension rather than acknowledge the limitations of comprehensive planning knowledge. Also, their capabilities are those required to perform an analytical, supportive, advisory role. Normally, they do not have the operating energy, constructive aggressiveness, decisiveness, or leadership qualities characteristic of successful line executives. If they did, serious incompatibility would almost certainly develop between staff planners and the line executives they serve.

A well-developed planning center is inherently impressive in what it attempts to do. The concentration of interesting information and the visual attractiveness and clarity of graphic expression often produce a desire on the part of executives to "show off" the mechanism, to make additional use of it for purely promotional or political purposes and to impress guests and visitors. This usually leads to "gold plating" the installation, incorporating costly features befitting its use by legislative decision-makers, chief executives, or boards of directors that add nothing to the quality of information and analysis. This is to be avoided at all costs, since it promotes presentations which are polished briefings rather than analytical explorations into the issue at hand. Last-minute changes or adjustments during meetings cannot be made if superficial beauty of presentation takes precedence. The "drafting room syndrome" referred to earlier in this book is reintroduced, with its time delays and added costs.

Planning centers are above all *work places,* where substance rather than deliberately impressive appearance is emphasized. This does not mean that displays are sloppy or unattractive. Quite to the contrary, the analyses themselves have an inherent order, clarity, and attractiveness regardless of the flexible and inexpensive materials used in their formulation or presentation. In fact, planning centers are most impressive if form follows function and they clearly reflect their purpose as work places.

Because of their preeminent management function and potential for impressive display, there is also a tendency to overstaff planning centers. In a place of concentrated activity that fulfills a complex function in a limited space, too many staff people occupying the center simply get in each other's way. Since preparatory analysis can be done elsewhere, surprisingly few personnel are required to maintain the city planning center itself. The quality and not the quantity of staff personnel is of paramount importance. As small as possible is likely to be most beautiful.

LEGAL MECHANISM

As now formulated in the United States, municipal master plans are recommendations by city planning departments and commissions to their legislatures to enact the laws and initiate the actions that effectuate these plans. The response of the legislative body can range from complete rejection to formal adoption which gives the master plan legal status as an acknowledged reference. If the plan is adopted, those concerned with the physical development of the city—for example, land developers, municipal agencies, and citizen groups—have more cause to challenge city council actions that violate a master plan than had no such acknowledgement been made.

The legislature is not obligated to follow a master plan unless it deliberately binds itself to conform with the plan and continues this commitment. At any time the legislature can override its self-imposed commitment to a plan, contending that conditions have changed, or that the public interest is better served by abandonment or modification of the plan. It is not possible to ensure legislative continuity and consistency by some form of legal mandate without at the same time dangerously restricting the freedom of legislative action essential in a democracy. Public and political pressures, and the actions necessary to meet a situation or respond to a need, are the major constraints on totally irresponsible legislative behavior.

Whether lawmakers and other elected municipal officials regard the master city plan as a firm commitment or a flexible guide depends on the political significance of the matter at hand. Other things being equal, elected officials attempt to retain the maximum possible freedom of choice and action, with the least commitment on their part. In this way, they reduce their identification with issues and actions that seem sound at the time of commitment, but under changed circumstances may haunt them at election time.

Planning departments, on the other hand, usually seek to make their plans unalterable, except in details, for as long as possible. Land developers, financial institutions, special interest groups, and individual citizens regard the master city plan as sacrosanct when it supports their desires of the moment. But when it does not, they claim it is only a very general guide that needs correction or revision, or it is a figment of the city planner's imagination which is irrelevant in the real world of urban development.

For these reasons, master plans are not yet institutionalized in the United States as a fundamental and formal part of municipal government. As they now exist, they do not represent what the municipality accepts as a definite commitment. For the most part, this is because the traditional end-state city plans proposed by city planning departments and commissions have been inadequate and unacceptable in ways discussed at some length earlier in this book. Until these invalidating deficiencies are resolved, the advisory status of master city plans should remain unchanged, and the persistent pressures of the federal government for bigger and better end-state city plans should be resisted. These pressures are simply compounding and perpetuating a fallacious concept.

Traditional city plans are composed of documents covering the proposed development of certain elements of the physical city. They are prepared by city planning departments and commissions who recommend them to city councils for adoption and implementing legislative action. City councils may choose to ignore these recommendations. They may accept them as a reference in whole or in part, but without formal acknowledgment of their source and without giving them any legal status. City councils may officially adopt city planning recommendations in whole or in part. They may regard the accumulation of their own legislative actions relating to land use and the physical-spatial development of the city as the master plan, independently from any recommendations by a city planning department or commission. Or they may consider the operating plans of the municipal departments to collectively comprise the master city plan.

The legislative actions and reference documents supporting any one of these possible forms of city planning by elected decision-makers constitutes the city plan. The file of legislative actions is kept by a city clerk, city recorder, or other official. Supporting documentation which is not directly part of legislative actions is maintained in the files of the city planning agency or it may be scattered among different municipal departments. The materials constituting the city plan can vary widely from city to city because of the functional differences between them and the different ways their city councils can conduct city planning.

The state enabling acts, which authorize local governments to conduct city planning under the police power, may require that city plans include particular elements such as land use, transportation, recreation, open space, or housing. This designation of required elements may be for a political purpose at the state level rather than logical selection in the best interests of communities throughout the state. The specific content or exact method of analysis for each element is not prescribed. How city plans are formulated and what they can and should include are the consequence of a host of forces and considerations: the character, needs, and resources of the community; the local political power structure; past history and future commitments; actions by other levels of government; and the effects on municipalities of events occurring beyond their borders. Realistic plans must evolve from within each community and reflect its structure and prospects. If outside motivation is justified to induce municipalities to formulate and use city plans, this should be provided by incentives and other encouragement free from rigid, unrealistic, or uncomprehending directives "from above."

As noted previously, almost all city plans in the United States are out of date because city council actions approving, denying, or modifying city planning matters are not reflected in published city plans for many months or even years. Zone changes are individually published as separate legislative acts in some official publication of record with limited circulation. The time required to publish a printed master plan precludes its being up to date when issued, unless no government actions are taken during the time it takes to produce the printed publication and the subsequent period of years before it is revised and republished. Such a prolonged moratorium of municipal action cannot be imagined in the real world of cities.

An end-state plan is legally indefensible, as well as operationally useless, if it is so immutable that it cannot incorporate modifications made necessary by municipal actions contrary to the plan as it was originally formulated. For example, the dynamics of urban development in the United States and most parts of the world almost guarantee that certain minor changes in land use will bring about an adjustment of plans for the immediately surrounding area. Some departures from land-use plans, modest in themselves, can have widespread consequences. A change of zone on a single small lot in a single-family district to a zone permitting apartments can lead, lot by adjacent lot, to the rezoning of a large area for multiple residential use. This in turn overloads municipal utilities and streets designed for the lower population density of single-family detached dwellings.

It is axiomatic that political and economic self-interests, as well as the dynamics of urban development, will continue to prevent strict adherence to rigid end-state plans. These plans, in turn, are unenforceable because they are predicated on there being no interim developments that could modify the desired outcome.

Initiation of continuous city planning as proposed in this book would encourage municipal legislatures to formulate realistic city plans as a basis for the coordination of departmental operations and plans, integration of citywide engineering systems, and the gradual resolution of urban problems requiring effective comprehensive planning and programs of progressive action.

Any legal difference between continuous planning and traditional planning as practiced today is a matter of degree and not of kind. The main difference is that the legal reference in continuous planning is not a printed master city plan but the recorded content of the city planning center. This includes the information and analysis on display panels, in use or in storage, photographic records of information collected and analysis performed in the past, and related city planning legislation and regulations. The official master city plan is that part of this material which has been adopted by proper authority, plus materials that support city planning regulations (which may be filed elsewhere). In time, the entire contents of the city planning center might constitute the master city plan.

Legal appeals from continuous city planning decisions require identification of the master plan and related regulations as they existed in the past. This is accomplished by a well-organized system of microfilm records of the display panels and other references that constituted the master plan at a particular point in the past. Essentially, this is what happens today, except that continuous city planning involves keeping track of more frequent changes.

If a document showing the current master plan is needed for distribution, it can be produced quickly by photographing the panels and relevant materials in the city planning center. These photographs can then be published as a printed document. This expense should be justified by a worthwhile purpose that can be served in no other way because, although the frequent modification characteristic of continuous city planning does not normally amount to continuous significant change, it does quickly outdate some part of the master plan.

Legal requirements of due process in city planning are met as successfully by continuous planning as by traditional planning. It is important, however, to substantiate that the more frequent changes involved in continuous planning are not arbitrary, but reflect new information, further analysis, or conditions calling for revision. This is best accomplished by carefully following planning procedures that ensure proper notification, public hearings, reasonableness, consistency, proper public purpose, and the opportunity for appeal.

STRATEGY OF USE

In the United States, planning faces fundamental difficulties inherent in the body politic, its legislative bodies, and society in general. Most of these difficulties apply to planning wherever conducted.

Recognizing and facing reality are fundamental to planning. Yet it is difficult to face unvarnished facts and unpleasant truths, and to avoid wishful thinking that is unconstructive or even destructive. As long as people are not forced by events to face an unpleasant reality, they prefer the comfort of an illusion to the nagging worry of a troublesome situation. Constant awareness of the accumulation of ever-present problems is more than most people can endure; understandably, they see no compelling reason why their existence should be so burdened. But the task of planning is precisely that of evaluating the real situation, however unwanted and unpleasant, and identifying problems and potential improvements.

Planning sets aside some of today's resources for use at some future time. But it is not easy for people to forego present needs and desires for future benefits that are probable but not certain, that they cannot enjoy because these benefits will accrue to a subsequent generation. Most people measure the desirability or undesirability of an endeavor and its success or failure in terms of their own lifetimes. Consideration of a distant and indefinite future is especially difficult for a materialistic society, which lacks the motivation provided indirectly in the past by greater concern with the hereafter. Much planning has been accomplished in the name of religion.

In general, people resist continual or extensive change. A minimum stability is necessary to avoid intolerable uncertainty and confusion concerning what is settled and what is still unresolved. The status quo is the most familiar and comfortable situation. But planning sets ever higher standards, calls for continuous improvement, and requires added effort. For the ordinary individual, it is easier to plan as little as possible rather than as much as suggested. Most people's energies are directed to their own personal problems and self-interests. For the vast majority, their days are consumed with meeting the demands of everyday living. Normally, they are concerned with city planning only when some urban development impinges directly and immediately on their lives.

All planning presupposes and requires the application of rationality rather than unfettered emotion, the triumph of order over disorder, of positive hope over enervating discouragement or fatalism, of constructive action over inaction. But behavior patterns and attitudes supportive of city planning are not characteristic of most people. They are attained only as a result of deliberate effort or strong motivation. The fact that people's natural tendencies must be surmounted or avoided for city planning to be successful is often forgotten or ignored by professional city planners in the United States.

Coordination of the various components of a city is also inherent in planning. But as previously noted, coordination does not come easily to people. Psychologically, people tend to live apart self-protectively. Inevitably, coordination implies less egocentrism, which history has amply demonstrated is not readily displayed. Nevertheless, not only coordination but close synthesis are basic to comprehensive planning.

Sooner or later, most organizations are affected in some way by an activity as broadly impactful as city planning. Financial institutions have large investments in urban land and real property, whose value relates to transportation facilities, utility services, zoning, or some other element of city planning. Changing the zone on land to what the owner invariably considers its "highest and best use" may increase its value many times. Commercial and industrial establishments depend for their location and success on available transportation for people and goods, utilities and services, housing for the workforce, and other elements of city planning. New developments must conform to land-use regulations, which relate to the financing and profitability of the planned project. Individual home owners react strongly when changes of land use are proposed in the immediate neighborhood that they believe will depreciate their property. In each of these examples, with very few exceptions, organizations and individuals involved will be against city planning when it affects their self-interests adversely.

In the light of these realities, neither the municipal citizenry nor its elected representatives can be expected to seek or embrace any form of effective city planning with immediate and enduring enthusiasm. Politicans may be temporarily enthusiastic if planning serves their self-interest, but as pointed out above this is not often. They may request city planning studies, not because they want the results for guidance, but because they believe that while the studies are being conducted the troublesome issue will be forgotten.

Normally, municipal decision-makers—politicians, executive officials, and governmental civil servants—do not want to commit themselves any more than necessary or more than their self-interest requires. The more numerous their options, the fewer their commitments or stated positions, the more room there is to maneuver in the arena of political and bureaucratic survival and advancement. For these reasons, regardless of need, it is unrealistic to expect continuous city planning to be welcomed even by those with the governmental responsibility of carrying it out.

A deliberate strategy of acceptance and use is required. First, it must be demonstrated that the self-interests of many people in municipal government are served by a core of reference information and analysis. Members of the city council, the mayor, and the city manager or administrative officer can use the information maintained in the city planning center to their own advantage as well as to better fulfill their responsibilities of directing the city. Municipal department and agency managers learn from the information contained in the center how the activities of other units relate to their operations and plans. Professional employees from different municipal departments can obtain specific data they need concerning the policies, longer-range plans, or operating programs of other city units. A gradual increase in use establishes the city planning center as a desirable mechanism, which some people may find too revealing at times but most people find frequently useful for their own self-interest.

For the different municipal departments to coordinate their activities, the core of information and analysis covering the current operations and future plans of each one must be available to the others, and to those who must decide among competing demands for available funds. While this coordination is usually resisted at first, it can be demonstrated that conflicting activities by different municipal units can no longer be afforded, that mutual support is to everyone's advantage in the long run, and that coordination is critical in today's world of interdependencies which were far less crucial not long ago.

Coordination requires that each department or agency of municipal government prepare its proposed budget and operating plan for the next year, its operating plan for the following five years, and any further plans for the longer-range future. Units that have not compiled the necessary data are assisted in doing so. The planning staff develops the information as best it can for units that do not cooperate; the disadvantage to the unit of this preemption of its self-determination is soon apparent.

Since information, analysis, decisions, and actions recorded in the city planning center constitute the legal master city plan, the center becomes a necessary reference for many municipal activities. City departments, the mayor, city manager, council members, city attorney, and others use it to determine, legally support, justify, or explain city planning decisions and implementing actions. Applicants for city planning approvals, special interests, citizens' groups, and litigants refer to it for the information each needs. Various private enterprises not directly involved in city planning find that following the information and analysis provided for continuous city planning enables them to improve the conduct of their own affairs. Such regular contact has not occurred in the past because analytical centers have not existed, and traditional city plans have not been significant enough to warrant such utilization and attention.

An important use of the city planning center is to evaluate alternatives. When the time comes periodically to consider the allocation of available resources among the many competing demands, a number of different resolutions are possible. Each alternative must be consistent within itself, but also meet the over-all limitations and requirements of the municipal situation as a whole. This is difficult to do without the information, analysis, and flexible means of comparison provided by a planning center.

For example, the proposals of different municipal departments regarding matters for which they are responsible but which also affect the operations and plans of other government units can be examined in the city planning center by all concerned. This should make the final form of departmental budgets, operating plans, and five-year plans more explicable and probably more acceptable. Certainly this procedure increases awareness of citywide planning and encourages participation by municipal departments in the formulation of the master city plan. When the consequences of individual departmental planning are examined and alternatives considered, the likelihood of irreconcilable disagreement is reduced. Since the information and analysis shown in the center indicates the parameters that feasible plans must meet, citizen groups can prepare advocacy plans realistic enough for careful consideration.

Administrative inefficiencies multiply disproportionately as urban bureaucracies grow bigger and bigger. They are motivated less toward public service than avoidance of difficult problems and controversies and become preoccupied with internal politics and administrative maneuvering for career advancement, job security, and plentiful pensions. Government becomes divorced from the citizenry and more responsive to special interest groups and pressures than to the public interest. In general, people in the United States resist city planning except when it serves them personally. This is not an encouraging scene, but it is by no means a hopeless one. Not only is it possible to marshall greater support for more effective city planning by proper strategies, but technological and environmental developments require coordination, and the federal government is becoming more insistent and persistent in its efforts to force improved city planning.

Progressive involvement is the key tactic in getting continuous city planning accepted gradually by municipal government and by the community generally. Item by item, information and analysis are made useful to decision-makers and the municipal powers that be. Their self-interests are deliberately served, with the further purpose of eventually associating these municipal officials with the continuous city planning process and staff. First, the information and analysis provided off and on by the planning staff are found reliable and useful by influential individuals. Next, formal procedures are established or informal ways are found for continuing this staff support. It becomes increasingly difficult for decision-makers to abandon what has become a familiar source of information and analysis. From a small beginning assisting municipal officials in connection with their own expressed interests, continuous city planning develops gradually until it becomes ingrained as a permanent part of municipal government. Something of the sort must have occurred in the past preceding the adoption of the budget: at first undoubtedly resisted as an intrusion, now a managerial-administrative fixture that cannot be ignored—although unfortunately it is occasionally manipulated to the point of misrepresentation.

COST

The personnel required for continuous city planning need be no more numerous nor more highly paid than those now engaged in traditional city planning. In fact, they should be fewer in number if the greater knowledge required of them is matched by increased efficiency. The number of people needed to formulate information and analysis on display panels and make photographic records will be more than offset by people no longer required for typing, drafting, and publication. People from various municipal offices may work in the city planning center from

time to time on information and plans that they develop. To the extent
that this reduces the work of the regular planning staff, operating costs
are reduced. Those engaged in the planning center who have worked in
traditional city planning may have to readjust their habits. Not only are
there profound differences in approach and philosophy, but continuous
city planning requires much greater alertness and quick responses to urban needs and events.

Costs of collecting information should be no more than for traditional
end-state plans. While it should be possible with continuous planning to
acquire and analyze more data that can be used in decision-making, the
cost should be no greater because of more efficient organization and
processing of the data. If more than this additional increment of information can be used effectively for continuous decision-making in a planning center designed for the purpose, the cost of collecting and
processing information will naturally be higher for the superior product.

It must be recognized that evaluating the costs and benefits of most
kinds of planning is difficult.

> In general . . . the higher the level of a corporate planning group, the
> less [the] likelihood that its activities can be measured in terms of specific
> savings. (McLean, 1961)
>
> I do not believe that one can usefully come up with dollar earnings or
> dollar savings attributable to the Long-Range Planning function. This is
> because usually the function is a necessity to the conduct of a business
> which survives, and the real question is whether it is formally recognized
> as a separate and distinct function or one which is joined with other func-
> tions and does not get clearly demarcated. (Bowman, 1961)

Of the many difficulties in evaluating planning, time lag and differen-
tiation are most significant. Since many of the benefits of comprehensive
planning do not manifest themselves for some time, today's record reflects planning analysis and decisions of the past. Usually, there is a time
lag of years between major city planning decisions and the returns (benefits) that permit an evaluation of their soundness. Since the fiscal year is
one year and there is a strong tendency to "let bygones be bygones" and
to concentrate on the present and future, the connection between past
analysis and decision and the current situation and present prospects is
rarely established. It is not surprising that quantification of cause and effect is seldom feasible when there are added to the problems of tracking
back past events the logical and cost-accounting difficulties of differen-

tiating the consequences of specific planning decisions from the many other factors involved.

Cost-benefit evaluation of planning is made all the more difficult because it is introduced most successfully and functions with the least friction when accomplishments of comprehensive planning are credited to the component units of the organization rather than to its central planning staff. Different municipal departments, for example, will more likely accept the concept of continuously coordinated operations and comprehensive planning for the city as a whole, if they consider its positive results to be a consequence of their actions. If as much of the credit for success as possible (and as little of the blame for mistakes) is associated with the departments, and they benefit thereby, their natural resistance to a higher-level coordination of plans is greatly reduced. This is achieved by working closely with each department to the point where it accepts any necessary revisions of its plans as justified and as the results of its own decision. On occasion, the central planning staff may accept the role of scapegoat to prevent disharmony.

If not carried to an extreme, this attributive approach is justified because the heads of municipal departments are responsible for the success or failure of their activities. When department heads are responsible for an accounting "cost center," they protect their prerogatives because administrative advancement is related to the record and image of achievement. Reluctant departmental managers can be induced to participate in continuous city planning, or replaced if they are persistently uncooperative; of course, this is neither desirable nor effective compared with gaining the cooperation of department heads by making it their show. A consequence of attributing credit to others is that the continuous city planning staff cannot claim credit for its own contributions except through the good offices of others.

Whether the net return on investment in planning justifies the cost is essentially a matter of judgment. Costs are easier to determine than benefits because they are limited by accounting definitions and tradition concerning what can be quantified; even valuable trademarks are assigned an arbitrary value of one dollar in corporate accounting. The salaries and overhead costs of staff planning personnel are readily calculated. The operating expenses of the city planning center can be established. Any reimbursable costs for specific studies or services performed by the central planning staff for other municipal cost centers are taken into account. Budgets can be set and enforced.

To obtain the total cost of continuous city planning, its budget is added to expenditures for coordinative planning by municipal departments that (1) were made in response to a request by the comprehensive planning staff, (2) are not part of the normal expense of efficient management of the department, or (3) exceed the expenditure for planning ordinarily expected by units of the city government. Exact accounting of the time and money required for continuous city planning is difficult, impractical, and prohibitively expensive. To distinguish among costs to be attributed to legislative decision-making, general management, and comprehensive city planning is never simple and clear-cut.

Since cost control is important, costs are usually of greatest concern to management. They are much easier to identify specifically and are much more immediately apparent than benefits. To evaluate costs and to exercise cost control, staff personnel can record how much time they spend on different activities; the expenses of operating the city planning center can be determined; and the person-hours required for various staff activities can be roughly evaluated by comparison with the known costs of comparable endeavors. But quantification of costs can never be conclusive because there are always hidden expenditures that are hard to specify in comprehensive planning.

Past expenditures and current commitments for comprehensive planning are hard facts, whereas benefits necessarily follow only after activities which involve costs. We accept the traditional accounting of administrative costs referred to in the previous paragraph, because it does not purport to be inclusive. Rarely, for example, is the executive time spent on a legislative, administrative, or planning endeavor fully recorded and accounted for. The comparative value of time expended on different managerial or planning activities cannot be precisely quantified, but only estimated. Nor can the dollar costs be calculated of using personnel in ways that do not fit their capabilities or their motivating interests. Certainly, the costs in time lost through mistakenly shortened careers and increased expenses of recruitment and training are not calculated. There are no standard costs of managerial ulcers or professional discontent.

Meaningful measurement has not been developed to compare the success of different methods of municipal management with respect to effective coordination of components, efficient communication, high morale, or favorable reputation. Nor is there an accurate way of measuring the outcomes of policies and decisions that cannot be evaluated for some time to come. In some cases, no measurement is possible because the outcomes of planning become so intermixed and obscured by subsequent events and changed circumstances.

In considering the costs and benefits of continuous city planning, expenditures are usually accepted at face value because they are expressed as "real numbers," but benefits are challenged unreasonably because they can only be estimated, forecast, or possibly evaluated more precisely at some future time when results are expected. Actually, as indicated, both sides of the cost-benefit accounting are inconclusive. Both involve the critical element of human judgment. The appraisal of benefits is less tangible and more difficult in degree rather than in kind.

In justifying continuous city planning, a burden of numerical proof which is unrealistic or impossible defeats its purpose. If benefits could be calculated as closely as costs, comprehensive city planning would not be conducted at the highest level of government, for it is top management in business, legislators, and chief government administrators who must cope with intangibles and uncertain projections. Directing a business enterprise or municipality is inevitably less precise than directing one of its parts. Therefore, for better or worse, informed judgment of the value of continuous city planning transcends as well as reflects quantitative data.

MEANS OF EVALUATION

There are only several ways of evaluating the benefits of continuous comprehensive planning. The first is so unsophisticated that its true worth is rarely recognized. A record or log is kept by the director or other chief official of the planning activity of instances when he or she believes comprehensive planning has benefited the municipality in some definite way. However approximate, an estimate of the monetary value of the analysis, recommendation, or decision is made. Even a conservative estimate of the value of the benefit usually exceeds the cost of the staff activity required to produce it.

At the time of the notation, the instances are clear enough to everyone concerned, although there may be differences of opinion concerning the monetary value attributable to the contribution of the planning unit. With the passage of time, memory is blurred and many events are not remembered exactly when a periodic evaluation of the planning activity is undertaken, or hard times require cost cutting. If, however, claimed contributions and their estimated benefits have been noted in a file or logbook as they occur—with the date, relevant facts, supporting explanation, and perhaps several attestations if available—they constitute a meaningful record.

Although this evidence is judgmental and circumstantial, most of the situations reported are not only familiar to the legislative body and municipal officials who approve the budget for continuous city planning, but they are so similar to their own areas of management concern that the reported contributions are meaningful to them despite the absence of precise quantification. Even if there has been a turnover of legislators and officials, there will usually be people who recall the situation or records relating to it. Normally, there is no need for the comprehensive planning staff to claim credit publicly or within the local government. It should suffice that those who are directly responsible for reviewing its activities know what the continuous city planning staff claims to have achieved. Of course, it never hurts to have the active support of officials in other units of municipal government, and of people outside government who find the comprehensive planning activity worthwhile for one reason or another.

Another means of appraisal is an ad hoc committee of from three to five persons who are competent and respected. They should be sufficiently experienced to be able to judge performance, with knowledge of planning generally and city planning specifically, and without vested or conflicting interest with respect to the role of the planning unit. They must be able to spend enough time to review operations in some detail. To this end, they should be reasonably compensated and reimbursed for their expenses.

The committee reports its collective or separate opinions with a clear explanation of the reasoning behind each of its conclusions. Of course, this evaluation is as subjective as individual opinion. Its merit lies in plural personpower, the probability that several well-chosen heads are better than one. Also, there is no direct involvement, which should make it easier for the committee members to be as objective as possible. In addition, their findings should always be useful to the director of the continuous planning activity, as a confirmation of the performance of the unit, or for the suggestions made which could lead to improvement.

Insofar as it can be done, the responsible director also evaluates his own management and operations. Although such self-evaluation is very difficult (and impossible for some people), the director can try to be as constructively objective as possible. Realistic self-appraisal, including deliberate self-criticism, is in the director's self-interest because it is to his advantage to improve performance.

The best evaluation would be the combination of all three of these means. With the log of claimed attainments, the observations and conclusions of an independent and competent committee, and the director's evaluation of his own and his staff's performance, there is a substantial basis for reliable appraisal.

REFERENCES

Bowman, Dean O. (Vice President, Long-Range Planning, Autonetics, Division of Northern American Aviation, Inc.), personal communication, 27 September 1961.

Branch, Melville C., *Planning: Aspects and Applications,* New York (Wiley), 1966, pp. 149, 147–148, 170–171.

Branch, Melville C., and Robinson, Ira, "Goals and Objectives in Civil Comprehensive Planning," *The Town Planning Review,* Vol. 38, No. 4, January 1968, pp. 261–267.

Brewer, Garry D., review of *New Tools for Urban Management* by Richard S. Rosenbloom et al, *Science,* Vol. 176, No. 4035, 12 May 1972, p. 648.

California Legislature, Senate Bill 1448, 13 May 1980.

Choay, Françoise, *The Modern City: Planning in the 19th Century,* New York (Braziller), 1969, p. 17.

Hill, Gladwin, "U.S. Lends a Hand in Restoring California's Stricken Desert," *The New York Times,* 11 May 1980, p. 8E.

Kamen, Joseph M. (Professor of Marketing, Indiana University Northwest), *The Wall Street Journal* (Letters to the Editor), 23 September 1971, p. 14.

Karachi Development Authority, with the assistance of the United Nations, *The Karachi Development Plan 1974–1985,* Final Report, Pilot Project 3, Karachi, Pakistan (Master Plan Department), August 1974, pp. vii, viii.

Kissinger, Henry, *White House Years,* Boston (Little, Brown), 1979, p. 34, 39, 602.

Lewis, Sylvia, "Florida's Cities Bite the Planning Bullet," *Planning,* Vol. 35, No. 2, February 1979, pp. 25, 26.

Lynn, Laurence E., Jr., "The Analyst as Craftsman," *Bulletin, John F. Kennedy School of Government,* Vol. III, No. 2, Fall/Winter 1979/80, pp. 38, 39.

McLean, John J. (Vice President, Continental Oil Company; later President and Chairman of the Board), personal communication, 11 September 1961.

Miller, Judith, "Feds Want a Closer Look at How Cities Keep Books," *The New York Times,* 13 May 1979, Section 4, p. E3.

Mills, Edwin S., "A Critical Evaluation of 'The Community Analysis Model,'"

Washington, D.C. (Department of Housing and Urban Development), HUD-PDR-363-3, January 1979, pp. 37, 44.

Netter, Edity, "Plan Status Changes," *Planning,* January 1980, p. 8.

Pearson, Robert C. (Vice President and Controller, Texas Instruments, Inc.), quoted by Linley H. Clark, Jr., in "Annual Overhaul: Zero Budgeting Is Being Used by Many Companies," *The Wall Street Journal,* Monday, 14 March 1977, p. 21.

Peterson, George E., "America's Urban Capital Stock: An Interview with George E. Peterson," *The Urban Institute: Policy and Research Report,* Vol. 10, No. 1, Spring 1980, p. 9.

A Plan for the City and Area of Grand Haven, Ottawa County, Michigan (Grand Haven Planning Commission and Scott Bagby & Associates of Grand Rapids), 1963, p. 58.

Rout, Lawrence, "Computer Choler, Many Managers Resist 'Paperless' Technology for Their Own Offices," *The Wall Street Journal,* 24 June 1980, pp. 1, 18.

Silk, Leonard, "The Game Theorist: Morgenstern Is Critical of Economics as Practiced," *The New York Times,* 13 February 1977, Section 3, p. F1.

Stuart, Reginald, "Study Finds Major Inadequacies in U.S. Cities' Financial Reports," *The New York Times,* 4 June 1979, p. D9.

Tight, Lieutenant General Eugent E., Jr., Opening Address, *Photogrammetric Engineering & Remote Sensing,* Vol. XLV, No. 6, July 1979, pp. 952, 954.

U.S. National Resources Committee, *Planning Our Resources,* Washington, D.C., March 1938, pp. 1, 2.

The Wall Street Journal, western edition, 18 April 1980, p. 14.

Wooldridge, Dean E., in Melville C. Branch, *The Corporate Planning Process,* New York (American Management Association), 1962, p. 15.

[Baron Georges Eugène] Haussmann's method of attack was as original as his task [as Prefect of Paris, to replan the system of boulevards for Napoleon III]. All decisions had first to be supported by analysis of the existing situation. His "initial studies" (to use the Prefect's own expression) are evidence against the a-priori reasoning of which he has been accused. . . . His first step on entering the Hôtel de Ville was to have drawn up a detailed and accurate plan of the whole city, the first of its kind. . . . When the surveys were completed, he had the plan engraved on large sheets . . . mounted on canvas and juxtaposed on a *frame on wheels,* forming a screen which never left his office. Haussmann constantly studied the plan, which complemented his firsthand knowledge of the city. . . .

Haussmann's documentation was not static, however. The Prefect understood that the city, like any organism, evolves in time, and that the view of the observer must therefore be at once prospective and retrospective, in order to safeguard its traditional dynamics as well as orienting the future. (Choay, 1969)

INDEX